CAMBRIDGE
UNIVERSITY PRESS

Click Start

INTERNATIONAL EDITION

Learner's Book 3

T0139663

CAMBRIDGE
UNIVERSITY PRESS

Shaftesbury Road, Cambridge CB2 8EA, United Kingdom

One Liberty Plaza, 20th Floor, New York, NY 10006, USA

477 Williamstown Road, Port Melbourne, VIC 3207, Australia

314–321, 3rd Floor, Plot 3, Splendor Forum, Jasola District Centre, New Delhi – 110025, India

103 Penang Road, #05-06/07, Visioncrest Commercial, Singapore 238467

Cambridge University Press is part of the University of Cambridge.

It furthers the University's mission by disseminating knowledge in the pursuit of education, learning and research at the highest international levels of excellence.

www.cambridge.org
Information on this title: www.cambridge.org/9781108951845

First published 2021

20 19 18 17 16 15 14 13 12 11 10 9 8 7 6 5 4

Printed in India by Multivista Global Pvt Ltd.

ISBN 9781108951845 Paperback

Introduction

The international edition of ***Click Start: Computing for Schools*** is designed around the latest developments in the field of computer science, information and communication technology. Based on Windows 7 and MS Office 2010, with extensive updates on Windows 10 and MS Office 2016, the series aids the understanding of the essentials of computer science including computer basics, office applications, creative software, programming concepts and programming languages.

Each level of the series has been designed keeping in mind the learning ability of the learners as well as their interests. Efforts have been made to use examples from day-to-day life, which will help the learners to bridge the gap between their knowledge of the subject and the real world. The books are designed to offer a holistic approach and help in the overall development of the learners.

KEY FEATURES

- **Snap Recap:** Probing questions to begin a chapter and assess pre-knowledge
- **Learning Objectives:** A list of the learning outcomes of the chapter
- **Activity:** Interactive exercise after every major topic to reinforce analytical skills and application-based learning
- **Exercise:** A variety of questions to test understanding
- **Fact File:** Interesting concept-related snippets to improve concept knowledge
- **Quick Key** and **Try This:** Shortcuts and useful tips on options available for different operations
- **Glossary:** Chapter-end list of important terms along with their definitions
- **You Are Here:** A summary for a quick recap
- **Lab Work:** Practical exercises to enable application of concepts through learning-by-doing
- **Project Work:** Situational tasks to test practical application of the concepts learnt
- **Who Am I?:** Biographies to inspire young learners
- **Sample Paper:** Practice and preparation for exams

The books make learning fun and help the learners achieve expertise in this fast-changing world of computer science.

Overview

Snap Recap
Probing questions to begin a chapter and assess pre-knowledge

SNAP RECAP
1. What are the basic parts of a computer?
2. Define input, storage and output devices. Also, give their examples.
3. What do you know about data and CPU?

Learning Objectives
A list of the learning outcomes of the chapter

LEARNING OBJECTIVES

You will learn about:
- IPO cycle
- hardware and software
- examples of hardware and software
- difference between hardware and software
- types of software
- operating system and its types

Activity
Interactive exercise after every major topic to reinforce analytical skills and application-based learning

ACTIVITY

Complete the following activity.
1. Make a document 'Myname.docx'.
2. Write a paragraph about yourself.
3. You will see your name will be showing a spelling mistake as our names are not part of the dictionary. Add your name in the Dictionary so that it doesn't show as an error in the next file.

EXERCISE

A.   State true or false.

1. The sleep option helps to save electricity.
2. Recycle Bin consists of copied files.
3. The Menu bar lists the tasks that a program can perform.
4. Vertical scroll bar appears below the Document area.
5. The Lock option can also shut down the computer.

Exercise
A variety of questions to test understanding

FACT FILE

Microsoft Windows is the most popular operating system. It runs on almost 90 per cent of the home computers in the world.

Fact File
Interesting concept-related snippets to increase concept knowledge

Quick Key
and **Try This**
Shortcuts and useful tips on options available for different operations

TRY THIS

Some software programs are also available for free on the Internet. List down at least five such examples.

Glossary
Chapter-end list of important terms along with their definitions

GLOSSARY

Change Case This is the option that changes the case of the written text.
Copy This is the option that creates a duplicate of the selected text.
Cut This is the option that is used to move the selected text from one position to another.
Find This is the option that searches word document for specified word(s).
Paste This is the option that places the Cut/Copy text at the required location.
Redo This is the option that repeats the last action performed.
Replace This changes the selected text with a new text.
Undo This is the option that reverses the last action performed.

You Are Here
A summary for a quick recap

YOU ARE HERE
4
1. Closed figures have no gaps between the lines that form them.
2. Open figures have gaps in the lines that form them.
3. Foreground colour is used for text, lines and borders of shapes.
4. Background colour is used for colouring closed figures and the background of text boxes.
5. You use Select to copy and paste a part of the picture.
6. To remove the last change you made to the file, click on the Undo button in the Quick Access Toolbar. To repeat the last action, click on the Redo button.

LAB WORK

A. Open the MSWLogo software on your computer. Observe how many Control buttons there are in the Commander window. Draw these buttons in Paint. Also using the Text tool, write the functions of the Execute and Halt buttons.
B. Practise opening and exiting the MSWLogo screen.
C. Using Paint, make the turtle of different colours, shapes and sizes.

Lab Work
Practical exercises to enable application of concepts through learning-by-doing

PROJECT WORK

Draw any 5 letters of the English alphabet in capital letters. An example is given here for your reference.

A, H, N, T, X

Outcome: You will be able to understand the turtle movement and will be able to decide the requisite number of steps and angle for drawing different figures.

Project Work
Situational tasks to test practical application of the concepts learnt

Sample Paper
Helps test learner understanding at the end of the course

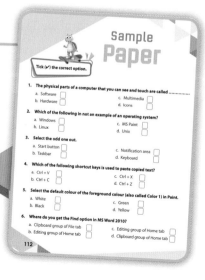

Sample Paper

Tick (✔) the correct option.

1. The physical parts of a computer that you can see and touch are called ....
   a. Software
   b. Hardware
   c. Multimedia
   d. Icons

2. Which of the following in not an example of an operating system?
   a. Windows
   b. Linux
   c. MS Paint
   d. Unix

3. Select the odd one out.
   a. Start button
   b. Taskbar
   c. Notification area
   d. Keyboard

4. Which of the following shortcut keys is used to paste copied text?
   a. Ctrl + V
   b. Ctrl + C
   c. Ctrl + X
   d. Ctrl + Z

5. Select the default colour of the foreground colour (also called Color 1) in Paint.
   a. White
   b. Black
   c. Green
   d. Yellow

6. Where do you get the Find option in MS Word 2010?
   a. Clipboard group of File tab
   b. Editing group of Home tab
   c. Editing group of Home tab
   d. Clipboard group of Home tab

112

WHO AM I?

I was born on 28 December 1969 in Finland. While using Minix (a Unix-like system) for educational purpose, I started writing my own kernel for Linux.

Linux was later combined with the GNU system which turned it into a freely available operating system.

I am ....

Who Am I?
Biographies to inspire young learners

Contents

01 Know Your Computer................................ 1
- ○ Input-Process-Output cycle (IPO cycle)
- ○ Differences between hardware and software
- ○ Types of software

02 Using Windows.................................... 10
- ○ Starting windows
- ○ Desktop
- ○ Icons
- ○ Gadgets
- ○ Components of a window
- ○ Accessories
- ○ Shutting down a computer

03 MS Word 2010 Interface 27
- ○ Components of the MS Word 2010 window
- ○ Inserting text in a document
- ○ Selecting text
- ○ Editing text
- ○ Undo and Redo options
- ○ Find and Replace
- ○ Spelling & Grammar
- ○ Change case

04 Using Paint Tools................................ 40
- ○ Shapes
- ○ How to fill color
- ○ More tools in Paint

05 Using the Text Tool in Paint 53
- ○ Text tool
- ○ Text tab
- ○ Components of the Text tab

06 Advanced Paint.................................. 64
- ○ Editing images
- ○ Image group
- ○ Resize and Skew
- ○ View tab

07 Tux Paint – Introduction 75
- ○ Features of Tux Paint
- ○ Starting Tux Paint
- ○ Components of the Tux Paint window
- ○ Drawing tools
- ○ Saving a picture
- ○ Opening a saved picture
- ○ Erasing a saved picture
- ○ Closing Tux Paint

08 MSWLogo – Introduction 90
- ○ Starting MSWLogo
- ○ MSWLogo window
- ○ Components of the MSWLogo screen
- ○ Components of the Commander window
- ○ Exiting MSWLogo

09 MSWLogo – Basic Commands 100
- ○ FORWARD command
- ○ BACKWARD command
- ○ RIGHT command
- ○ LEFT command
- ○ HOME command
- ○ SETH command
- ○ CLEARSCREEN command
- ○ CLEARTEXT command
- ○ HIDE TURTLE command
- ○ SHOW TURTLE command
- ○ REPEAT command
- ○ BYE command
- ○ Help tips for Logo

Sample Paper.................................. 112

Know Your Computer

SNAP RECAP

1. What are the basic parts of a computer?
2. Define input, storage and output devices. Give examples.
3. What do you know about data and the CPU?

LEARNING OBJECTIVES

You will learn about:
- the IPO cycle
- hardware and software
- examples of hardware and software
- the differences between hardware and software
- types of software
- types of operating system

Input-Process-Output Cycle (IPO Cycle)

Computers are human-made machines. They are used to do many things. For example, solve sums, listen to music, draw pictures, play games, etc. Computers function in the following way:

1. You enter data, facts or instructions into a computer using the keyboard or the mouse. This data or instruction is called **input**.

2. The computer converts the data into meaningful information with the help of the CPU. This step is called **processing**.

3. After processing the data, the computer gives you the result on the monitor. You can also take a printout of this result. This result is called the **output**.

Therefore, a computer may be defined as an electronic device that accepts data, processes it and gives the result. It follows a cycle which is known as

the **Input–Process–Output Cycle (IPO Cycle)**. This cycle is shown below.

Input-Process-Output cycle

Hardware and software

A computer system can be divided as follows.

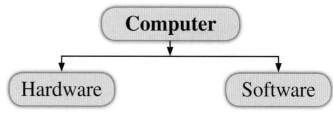

Different parts of a computer system

Hardware

The physical parts of a computer that you can see and touch are called **hardware**. The Central Processing Unit (CPU) is an example of hardware. There are more parts inside the CPU which you can see only when you open the CPU box. Other types of hardware are connected to the CPU using wires and cables.

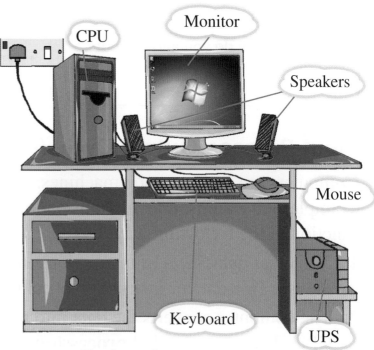

Hardware in a computer system

Uses of hardware are as follows:

1. the Monitor is used for displaying pictures.
2. the Keyboard is used for typing text.
3. the Mouse is used for giving instructions.
4. the Printer is used for printing pictures and documents.

Joystick, microphone, scanner and speakers are other examples of hardware.

Software

To understand what software is, let us take an example of a television (TV).

The TV itself is hardware but the programs you watch on it are software.

The set of instructions that tells the hardware how to perform a particular task is called a **Program**. All programs are **software**. Unlike hardware, we cannot see or touch software.

A boy watching TV

A computer needs software to work. Without software, a computer would be of no use.

There are different kinds of software to do different kinds of work on a computer. For example, Paint is a software program used for drawing and coloring pictures.

TRY THIS

Some software programs are also available for free on the Internet. Write down five examples.

Microsoft Word (MS Word) is a software program used for creating text documents. These software programs are readily available and can be bought and installed on your computer.

Differences between hardware and software

You already know that hardware are parts of the computer you can see and touch. Software is the set of instructions that tells the hardware how to perform a particular task. However, there is one more important difference between hardware and software.

Do you remember that a computer follows the Input–Process–Output cycle to perform tasks? Can you guess which parts of this cycle relate to hardware and which to software?

It is hardware that performs the input and output tasks (or operations). For example, you need a scanner to copy a picture on a computer, while for printing a picture you need a printer.

Input through hardware

Output through hardware

It is the software that does the processing tasks (or operations). Therefore, the hardware supports the input and the output and the software supports the processing part of the IPO cycle.

ACTIVITY

Rewrite the following jumbled words.

1. PCRUEOTM   ....
2. WAHRARED   ....
3. PTOUTU   ....
4. ESWOAFRT   ....
5. TPINU   ....

Types of software

There are two types of software.

| Application software | System software |

Application software

Software that is used to perform a specific task is called **application software**. Commonly used application softwares are discussed below.

Word processing software

These software programs are used to write letters, stories, reports, etc. The things you write with a pen can also be written with word processing software using a keyboard. The most commonly used word processing software is MS Word.

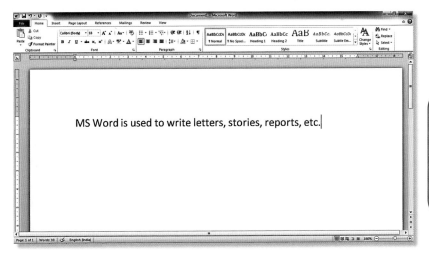

TRY THIS

Open MS Word and type two sentences about your school.

MS Word – A word processing software

Multimedia software

These software programs are used for drawing pictures, playing games and watching movies. Paint is a very simple kind of multimedia software.

A multimedia game

System software

Software that is used to control the operation of a computer is called **system software**. System software is needed to run the computer. It refers to the files and programs that make up your computer's **operating system**.

Operating system

The operating system controls the overall working of the computer. It manages the hardware and the software programs.

To understand what an operating system is, think of it as a traffic policeman. A traffic policeman tells cars and motorcycles when to move, in which direction and at what speed. In the same way, an operating system tells the computer when to run which software program and at what speed.

A traffic policeman directing traffic

There are many different types of operating systems. The most commonly used operating systems are Microsoft Windows and Mac OS. Some operating systems are also available for free, for example, Linux and Unix.

There are two types of operating system: *single-user operating system* and *multi-user operating system*.

FACT FILE

Microsoft Windows is the most popular operating system. It runs on almost 90 per cent of the home computers in the world.

Single-user operating system

Only one user can work on a single-user operating system at a given time. Microsoft Windows and Mac OS are both single-user operating systems. Such operating systems are mostly used at home.

Multi-user operating system

Many users can work on a multi-user operating system at the same time or even at different times. For this, one main computer is attached to many other computers. Unix and Linux are both multi-user operating systems. These are mostly used in big offices where there are lots of computers.

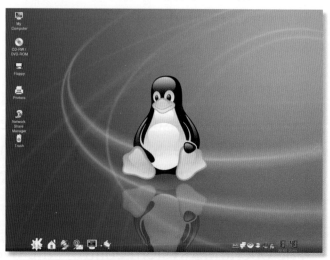

Linux operating system

Identify and color the different types of software programs in the grid below.

A	F	B	O	O	M	A	P	S
L	I	N	U	X	S	Y	A	M
M	W	S	N	Y	W	I	I	A
S	O	O	I	F	O	O	N	C
O	D	R	X	S	R	Y	T	O
M	S	W	I	N	D	O	W	S
J	I	S	F	A	Y	T	R	W

GLOSSARY

Hardware These are the physical parts of a computer that you can see and touch.

IPO cycle This stands for Input–Process–Output cycle.

Operating system This controls the overall working of a computer.

Software This is the set of instructions that tells the hardware how to perform a particular task.

YOU ARE HERE

1

1. A computer is an electronic device. It accepts data, processes it and then gives the result. This is called the IPO cycle.

2. A computer system can be divided into hardware and software.

3. Without software a computer would be of no use.

4. There are two types of software: Application software and System software.

5. There are two types of operating systems: Single-user operating system and Multi-user operating system.

EXERCISE

A. Find the missing letters to fill in the blanks.

1. Operations done by software.   __ R __ C __ __ S __ __ __

2. These are the parts of the computer that you can touch and feel.
   __ A __ D __ __ __ __

3. The result the computer gives after processing the data.   O __ __ __ __ __

4. The set of instructions that tells the hardware how to perform a particular task.   S __ __ __ __ A __ E

5. A very simple kind of multimedia software.   __ A __ __ __

B. True or false?

1. An operating system is a type of software.

2. Output is the data that you enter into a computer.

3. Linux is a type of application software.

4. Unix and Linux are both single-user operating systems.

5. MS Windows is an application software.

C. Match the following.

1.	Hardware		a.	Output
2.	Input–Process–		b.	Keyboard
3.	Processing		c.	Paint
4.	Software		d.	Data entered into the computer
5.	Input		e.	CPU

D. Answer the following questions.

1. What is meant by the Input–Process–Output cycle?
2. Define software.
3. Give two examples of hardware and software.
4. Define system software with an example.
5. What are the different kinds of operating systems?

LAB WORK

A. Go to the computer lab and use a software program like Microsoft Word to make a list of different kinds of hardware you find in the lab.

B. Draw two input devices and two output devices using Paint.

PROJECT WORK

In a group, create a 3D model of a computer showing hardware, software, operating system, input, output, storage devices, etc. Draw icons on the monitor using reusable boxes.

WHO AM I?

I was born on 24 February 1955 in California, U.S.

I am known as the co-creator of Macintosh, iPod, iPhone, etc.

In 1985, I left Apple Inc. and started a new software and hardware enterprise called NeXT.

I am ....

Using Windows

SNAP RECAP

In your computer lab, find out which operating system is being used. List all the icons available on the desktop. Also, find out the applications that are shown on the taskbar.

LEARNING OBJECTIVES

You will learn about:
- the desktop
- the taskbar
- icons
- components of a window
- shutting down a computer

This chapter uses examples from Windows 7. For Windows 10 updates, go to the end of the chapter.

Starting Windows

When you switch on a computer, all its parts are checked and you hear a beep sound. Then, the operating system is loaded in the computer's memory from its hard disk. This process is called **booting**. It remains in the memory until the system is on.

Starting Windows

FACT FILE

Microsoft Windows has different versions like Windows XP, Windows Vista, Windows 7 and Windows 8.

Windows 10 is the latest operating system from Microsoft.

Desktop

The Desktop is the first screen you see after booting. It consists of the **Taskbar** and **Icons**.

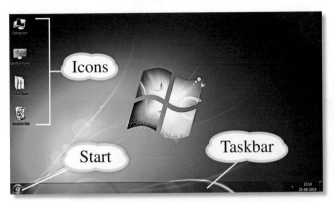

Different parts of the desktop

Taskbar

The taskbar is the long bar at the bottom of the desktop.

You will now learn about the different parts that make up the taskbar.

Start Button

The Start button is usually found on the extreme left of the taskbar. As the name suggests, you can start/begin working on a computer by clicking on this button.

When you click on the Start button, it opens a menu or a list. This is called the **Start menu**. It can be used to:

1. view a list of the software programs, applications and documents installed on the computer.
2. change the computer settings or shut down the computer.

3. Some of the items in the Start menu have a small arrow-head next to them. Holding the mouse pointer over these items opens another list. This is called a **Submenu**. The **Back** button with back-arrow can be used to go back to the main menu.

TRY THIS

Press the Windows key 🪟 on the keyboard to open the Start menu.

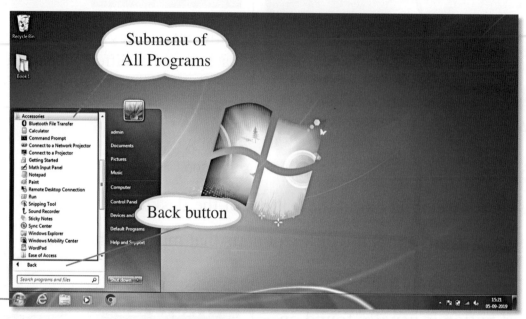

All Programs submenu

Keep track of your Windows

The **middle section** of the taskbar shows the programs and documents that have been opened.

Windows displays a button as an icon on the taskbar each time you open a program, application or document.

You can work on multiple programs, applications and

Each program has its own icon on the taskbar

documents at the same time. Icons of each of these will be displayed on the taskbar. This allows you to switch between opened windows or choose to work with multiple windows at the same time, which is very helpful.

In the screenshot on the previous page, multiple programs are open, for example, Paint, Calculator, etc. Each window has its own button on the taskbar.

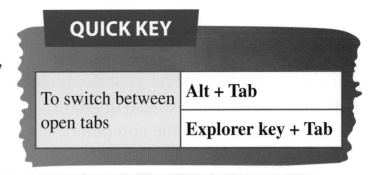

The button which is highlighted in the taskbar shows the active window.

Notification area

The notification area is on the right side of the taskbar. It contains small icons that give information about the status of the programs running on the computer at any given time. For example, battery life, sound status, date and time display, etc.

The notification area also includes the volume bar. If you keep the mouse pointer over the volume bar, it will show the volume indicator of the computer speakers.

Icons

As you have learnt, icons are the small pictures on the desktop. These are used to open software programs, etc. Desktop icons are also called **shortcuts**. The icons found on the desktop include Computer, Control Panel and Recycle Bin. Your desktop may have fewer or more icons.

Double-click the icon on the desktop to open the program or application. You may also use the keyboard to select the icons. Use arrow keys on the keyboard to go to a specific icon and then press the Enter key.

Computer icon

This icon displays the content of the computer. It shows the drives available for working.

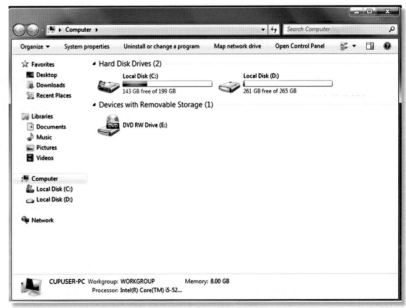

Using the Computer icon

13

Network icon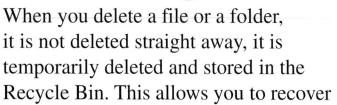

This helps you to connect your computer with other computers. It also displays the information about the computers connected to yours.

Using Network icon

Recycle Bin icon

When you delete a file or a folder, it is not deleted straight away, it is temporarily deleted and stored in the Recycle Bin. This allows you to recover your files/folders if they have been deleted by mistake.

Using the Recycle Bin icon

TRY THIS

Select a file or a folder to be deleted. Press **Shift + Del** keys. This will delete your file permanently.

Gadgets

Gadgets are mini-programs that appear on the desktop in Windows 7. These gadgets offer information at a glance. They also provide easy access to frequently used tools. Some of the gadgets that come with Windows 7 are Calendar, Clock, Weather, Feed Headlines, Slide Shows and Picture Puzzle.

Gadgets

Components of a window

Every software program opens in a **window**. The contents of every window are different. But most of them have some basic parts. Let us learn about the components of a window.

FACT FILE

Notepad is a simple text editor for Microsoft Windows. It is a basic text-editing program which enables computer users to create documents.

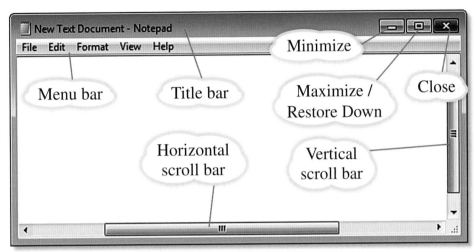

Components of a window

Title bar

The bar at the top of a window is called the Title bar. It shows you the name of the document and the software program.

Title bar

The Title bar has some important buttons. These are explained below.

Minimize button

Clicking the Minimize button reduces the window to an icon on the taskbar. Clicking that icon on the taskbar brings the window back to its original size.

Restore Down button

Clicking the Restore Down button reduces the window to a smaller size.

Maximize button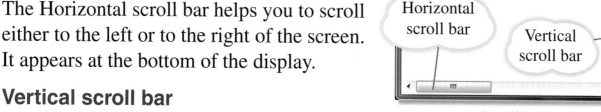

When the window becomes smaller, the Restore Down button is replaced with the Maximize button. Clicking the Maximize button increases the window to its full size.

Close button

Clicking this button closes the window.

Menu bar

The Menu bar is found just below the Title bar. It displays the menu names. These can be clicked to open different options available to use with the contents of the window.

Scroll bar

The Scroll bar lets you scroll the contents of the window to see information that is currently out of view.

Horizontal scroll bar

The Horizontal scroll bar helps you to scroll either to the left or to the right of the screen. It appears at the bottom of the display.

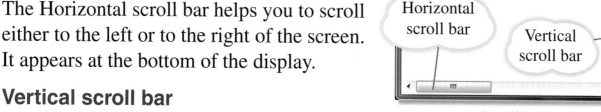

Scroll bars

Vertical scroll bar

The Vertical scroll bar helps you to scroll either to the top or the bottom of the screen. It appears on the right of the display.

Status bar

The bar at the bottom of the window is called the Status bar. It provides helpful information about the task that you are doing or the tool that you are using. The Status bar is not found in the Notepad program, but is available in other programs like MS Word.

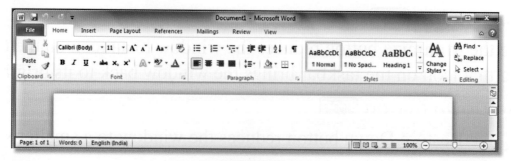

Status bar

Snap is a special feature of Windows 7. It allows you to resize the open window.

- You can drag the Title bar of an open window to either side of the desktop and resize it.
- You can drag a small-sized window to the top of the desktop to maximise that window.

Accessories

Windows 7 offers different types of Accessories to its users.

To open Accessories, click the **Start** button, go to **All Programs** and select **Accessories**.

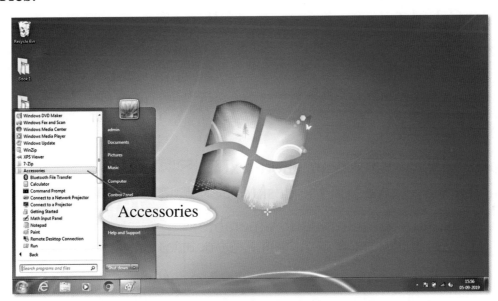

Opening Accessories

A variety of programs are found in Accessories that can be used for different purposes in our day-to-day life.

You have already learnt about Paint. You will now learn about other accessories.

Calculator

Have you seen a calculator in your home? It is used to do calculations like addition, subtraction, multiplication and division. It can also be used to perform more complex calculations.

You will find Calculator in the Accessories submenu of Windows 7.

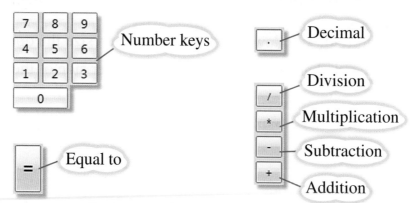

Buttons on the Calculator

The calculations are done by left-clicking on the buttons with a mouse or by typing numbers using the keyboard. For example, to add two numbers, say 8 and 2, follow these steps.

1. Open the Calculator.
2. Press 8.
3. Press the '+' symbol.
4. Press 2.
5. On pressing the 'equal to' button, the sum (that is, 10) will be seen on the Calculator screen.

Sticky notes

Sticky notes allow you to create short text notes which are displayed on the desktop.

You can use them to set reminders, timetable for study, etc.

TRY THIS

Right-click on the sticky note and choose a different color.

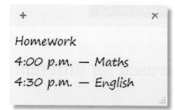

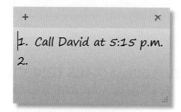

FACT FILE

The **Help and Support** option is found in the **Start** menu in Windows 7. When you click on this link, you will find information about a number of issues and topics related to Windows 7.

Shutting down a computer

After you have finished your work on the computer, always remember to shut down the computer correctly.

Steps to shut down a computer

These instructions are for Windows 7. For Windows 10 updates, go to the end of the chapter.

Step 1: Click on the **Start** button.

Step 2: Click on the **Shut down** option.

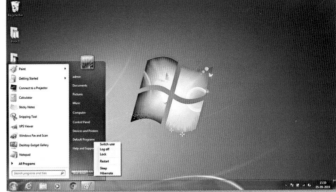

This will close all open programs, shut down Windows and then turn off your computer.

When you click on the arrow pointing to the right of Shut down, the following list of options are seen.

Shutting down the computer

Switch User

This helps to switch between different users without closing your programs.

Log Off

This closes programs and helps to log off from the current user session.

Lock

This locks the computer when the computer is not in use.

Restart

This closes all open programs, shuts down Windows and then starts Windows again.

Sleep

This saves the session and puts the computer in low-power state. With this, you can quickly resume your work.

Hibernate

This saves all your currently open documents onto the hard disk and then turns off the system. This option has been developed for laptops.

Solve the crossword using the clues given below.

Across

3. Mini-programs that appear on the desktop in Windows 7 are ....

6. Clicking the .... button reduces the window to a button on the taskbar.

7. .... gives you a list of the software programs, applications and documents on the computer.

8. The long bar at the bottom of the desktop is the ....

9. The bar at the bottom of the window is called the .... bar.

Down

1. The first screen we see after turning on a computer is ....

2. .... saves the session and puts the computer in low-power state.

4. Another name for Desktop icons is ....

5. .... saves all your currently open documents onto the hard disk and then turns off the PC.

Desktop   This is the first screen you see after you turn on the computer.

Gadgets   These are mini-programs that appear on the desktop.

Hibernate   This saves all your currently open documents onto the hard disk and then turns off the PC.

Horizontal scroll bar   This helps you to scroll the window to the left and to the right.

Icons   These are the small pictures on the desktop used for opening applications.

Menu bar   This displays the menu names.

Notification area   This gives the status of programs running on the computer.

Recycle Bin   This contains deleted files.

Start menu   This lists the programs, applications and documents on the computer.

Status bar   This gives information about the task or the tool being used.

Taskbar   This is the long bar at the bottom of the desktop.

Title bar   This shows the name of the document and the software program in use.

Vertical scroll bar   This helps you to scroll in upward and downward directions.

YOU ARE HERE

2

1. The operating system remains in the memory of the computer until it is switched on.

2. The Taskbar includes the Start button, Notification area, Date and Time.

3. The Start button opens the Start menu which lists the programs, applications and documents on the computer.

4. The Notification area shows the speed of the Internet connection.

5. Every software application opens in a window.

6. The Title bar, Menu bar, Document area, Scroll bars and Status bar are the basic parts of a window.

7. The Title bar includes the Minimize, Restore Down/Maximize and Close buttons.

8. The Scroll bar move the contents of the window up, down, left, or right to show information that is out of view.

9. To shut down a computer, click: Start ⟹ Shut down

EXERCISE

A.   True or false?

1. The sleep option helps to save electricity.

2. The Recycle Bin contains copied files.

3. The Menu bar lists the tasks that a program can perform.

4. The Vertical scroll bar appears below the Document area.

5. The Lock option can also shut down the computer.

B.   Fill in the blanks with the correct word.

1. .... are small pictures on the desktop for opening applications.

2. The .... allows you to switch between two windows.

3. All the deleted files remain in ....

4. .... scroll bar helps you to scroll the window in the left and the right directions.

5. Clicking the .... button reduces the window to a smaller size.

6. .... option allows you to create short text notes which are displayed on the desktop.

C. Match the following.

1. Explorer key + Tab   a. Speed of the Internet connection

2. Shift + Del   b. Title bar, Menu bar, Document area, Scroll bars and Status bar

3. Start ⟹ Shut down   c. To delete your file permanently

4. Notification area   d. To shut down a computer

5. Basic parts of a window   e. To switch between open tabs

D. Label the parts of the Title bar.

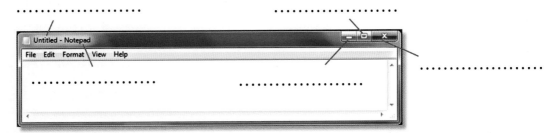

E. Answer the following questions.

1. What are the different components of a Taskbar?
2. What is the advantage of the Recycle Bin?
3. What are icons? Give two examples.
4. Explain various options available while shutting down a computer.
5. Can you open software programs with a single click? If yes, how?

LAB WORK 🖥

A. Use sticky notes to list the steps for working in Paint, including how to open, work and close the application.

B. Spot 3 gadgets in your computer (not mentioned in this book) and list their uses. Use different colored sticky notes for each of the 3 gadgets.

PROJECT WORK

Create a replica of the screen of your computer with icons and the taskbar, and add labels.

WHO AM I?

I was born on 28 December 1969 in Finland.

While using Minix (a Unix-like system) for educational purposes, I started writing my own for Linux.

Linux was later combined with the GNU system which turned it into a freely available operating system.

I am ....

24

- In Windows 10, the purpose of the desktop is similar to that of Windows 7 but they look different. The **Computer** icon of Windows 7 is replaced with **This PC**.

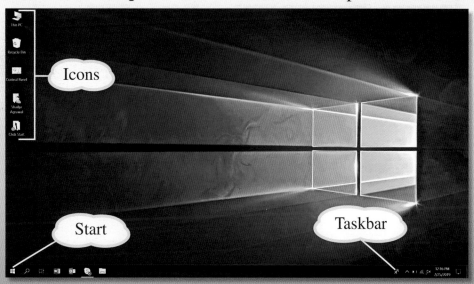

- All the applications are arranged alphabetically in the Start menu. All Programs and Accessories are no longer a part of Start menu. For quick access, the frequently used software applications are available in the taskbar of Windows 10.

- To shut down your computer, click on **Start** button ⟹ **Power** button ⟹ **Shut down**. You can also put your system in **Sleep** mode or **Restart** your computer from here.

- In Windows 10, the Recycle Bin looks like this:

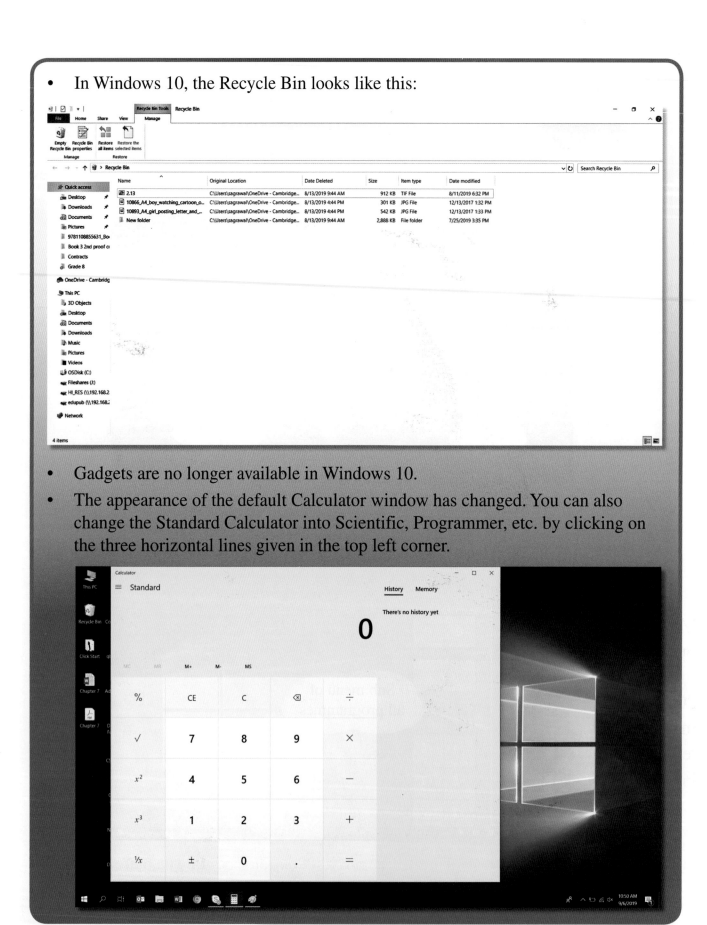

- Gadgets are no longer available in Windows 10.
- The appearance of the default Calculator window has changed. You can also change the Standard Calculator into Scientific, Programmer, etc. by clicking on the three horizontal lines given in the top left corner.

MS Word 2010 Interface

SNAP RECAP

1. What is Microsoft Word and where is it used?
2. Write the steps to start MS Word 2010.
3. Explain the components of the MS Word 2010 window.

LEARNING OBJECTIVES

You will learn about:

- the components of the MS Word 2010 window
- inserting, selecting and editing text
- using the Find and Replace options
- using the Undo and Redo options
- using Spelling & Grammar
- changing case

Introduction

Microsoft Word (MS Word) is a word processing software. There are numerous options available for presenting your text. This chapter will help you learn several important features in MS Word 2010 that will allow you to insert, edit, modify and display text (and non-text) components. For MS Word 2016 updates, go to the end of the chapter.

Components of the MS Word 2010 window

Let us revise the components of the MS Word 2010 window.

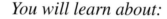
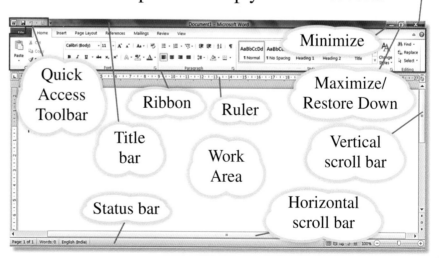

Components of the MS Word 2010 window

Components	Definition
Quick Access Toolbar	Contains some commonly used options like Undo, Redo and Save. More options can be added to it from the Ribbon.
Title bar	Displays the document name followed by the name of the application software. There are three control buttons present on the right of the Title bar: Minimize, Maximize/Restore Down and Close.
Ribbon	This is divided into tabs, which are further divided into groups. Some of the tabs on the Ribbon are: File, Home, Insert and Page Layout. Each group has a number of options that are used in MS Word 2010.
Ruler	Used to change the length and the width of a page margin.
Status bar	Provides information regarding page number, word count, language, page layout and zoom slider.
Scroll bars	These are used for viewing different areas of an active window. Two types of scroll bars are the Horizontal scroll bar and Vertical scroll bar.
Work Area	The area in the document where you can type the text.
Cursor	The blinking vertical line in the Work Area where the text will be typed.

Inserting text in a document

To begin writing in MS Word, left-click on the blank screen and begin typing using the keys on the keyboard. The text appears where the blinking cursor is located and the cursor starts shifting to the right of the text inserted. If you want to add text in between words you have already typed, then move the cursor to the desired location in your document using arrow keys, or left click on the location. Words/letters on the right will shift automatically to accommodate the text being added.

Inserting text in a document

Selecting text

Selecting text using a mouse

Select text when you want to move it to some other place or make a copy of it. Follow the steps given below to select text.

1. Position your mouse pointer on the text.
2. Keep the left click button pressed down and drag the mouse in the desired direction.
3. Drag it left, right, up or down to select the desired text/object.
4. When the text is selected you will see it highlighted with a colored band as shown.

Selected text

Selected text in a MS Word 2010 document

Editing text

The text can be edited by using the **Cut**, **Copy** and **Paste** options in the **Home** tab.

Cut

The Cut option is used to move the selected text/object from one position to another. It is followed by the Paste option to move the selected text/object to a new place/position.

The selected text is removed when you use the Paste option.

1. Select the desired text.
2. Click on the **Home** tab and select the **Cut** option from the **Clipboard** group.

Copy

The Copy option is used to copy the selected text/object to another place/position. It is followed by the Paste option to copy the selected text/object to another place/position.

The selected text is NOT removed when you use the Paste option and can be used multiple times. This is different from the **Cut** option.

1. Select the text to be copied.
2. Click on the **Home** tab and select the **Copy** option from the **Clipboard** group.

ACTIVITY

1. Write five sentences about today in MS Word.
2. Select the word 'today' from the first sentence, copy it and paste whenever you want to write the word 'today'.
3. Change the position of the second sentence by using the Cut option and use the Paste option to move this sentence to become the fourth sentence.
4. Save the document by giving it a name and save as '. docx' in the Documents folder.

Paste

Both the Cut and Copy options place the text/object on the Clipboard. To place it at the required position you need to use the Paste option. It works with both the Cut and Copy options.

QUICK KEY

Cut	**Ctrl + X**
Copy	**Ctrl + C**
Paste	**Ctrl + V**

1. Select the text. Use either the **Cut** or **Copy** option.
2. Place the cursor at the desired location where the text/object needs to be copied or moved.
3. Select the **Paste** option in the **Clipboard** group of the **Home** tab.

You can use the editing tools from the shortcut menu that opens when you right click on the selected text.

Undo and Redo options

To reverse the last action performed, click the **Undo** button on the **Quick Access Toolbar**. Click the **Redo** button to repeat the last action performed.

QUICK KEY

Undo	**Ctrl + Z**
Redo	**Ctrl + Y**

Find and Replace

The MS Word 2010 document can be easily searched for a particular word, phrase or a sentence by using the Find option. You can also replace the found text with some new text by using the Replace option. Follow the steps below.

1. Select the **Find** option in the **Editing** group of the **Home** tab.

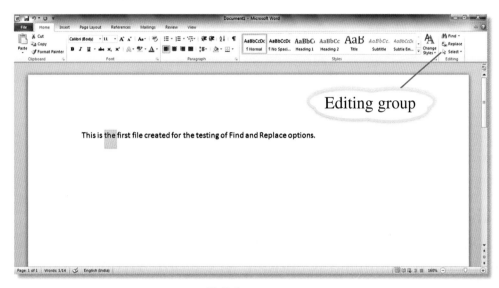

Editing group

The **Find and Replace** dialog box opens.

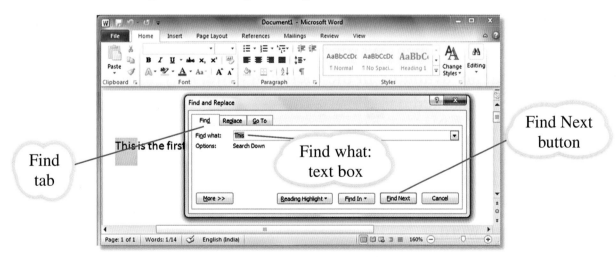

Find and Replace dialog box

2. Type the text to be searched in the **Find what** text box.
3. Click on the **Find Next** button. MS Word 2010 will start searching for the text in the document from the insertion point. If a match is found, MS Word 2010 stops searching and selects the text.
4. The search can be continued until the entire document is scanned.

5. To replace the selected text with some other text, click on the **Replace** option in the **Editing** group of the **Home** tab. Again, the **Find and Replace** dialog box appears.

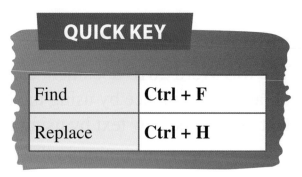
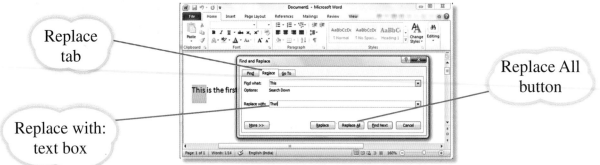

Replace tab

Replace All button

Replace with: text box

Find and Replace dialog box

6. Type the new text in the **Replace with** text box.
7. Click on either the **Replace** or **Replace All** button.
8. If **Replace All** command is chosen, MS Word 2010 will tell you the total number of replacements made. Click **OK**.

Spelling & Grammar

MS Word 2010 has an automatic spellchecker. It is used for correcting spellings as they are typed. Words typed in the document are compared to the ones that are available in the dictionary file. Any word that is not in the dictionary is marked as incorrect. All spelling mistakes on the document are underlined with a red wavy line (〰〰).

1. To correct a word, right click on it.
2. A shortcut menu pops up which displays the suggested spellings.

Correcting spellings in a MS Word 2010 document using the shortcut menu

3. Select the correct option from the shortcut menu.
4. If you feel that the word you have typed is correct, then click on **Ignore All**.
5. You can also add the word to the dictionary by using **Add to Dictionary**, so that next time it does not mark it as an incorrect spelling.

There is a feature in MS Word 2010 that enables it to correct common typing errors automatically. For example, if the user types 'teh', MS Word 2010 will automatically correct it to 'the'. If the automatic Spelling & Grammar check is not turned on, then follow these steps:

1. Click on the **Review** tab.
2. Click on the **Spelling & Grammar** option in the **Proofing** group.
3. The **Spelling & Grammar** dialog box appears.
4. The **Not in Dictionary:** section highlights the incorrect spellings and the **Suggestions** section suggests alternatives.
5. If you choose an option from the **Suggestions** list, click **Change** or ignore it by clicking **Ignore Once**.

You can also add and remove words on the **AutoCorrect** list.

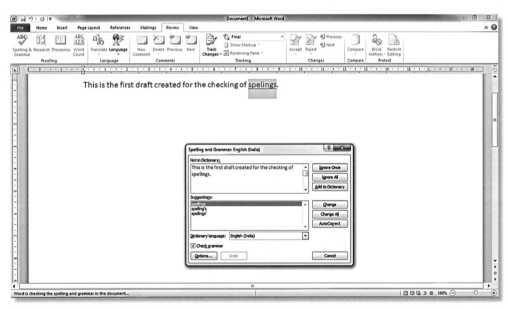

Correcting spellings in a MS Word 2010 document using the Review tab

6. When the spelling and grammar has been checked in the entire document, a **Microsoft Office Word** dialog box appears. Click **OK**.

Change Case

The Change Case option enables you to change the case of the written text. There are five options available that help you to change the case of the selected text.

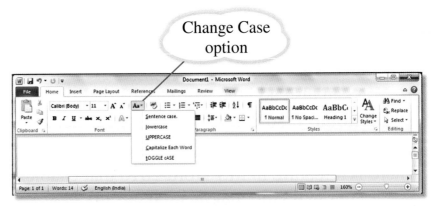

Change Case option in Home tab

Sentence case

The first character of every sentence is converted into UPPER CASE.

Upper case

All the selected text is converted into UPPER CASE.

Lower case

All the selected text is converted into lower case.

Capitalize Each Word

The first character of every word is in UPPER CASE.

Toggle case

It changes the selected text into reverse case, that is, lower case is converted into UPPER CASE and vice versa.

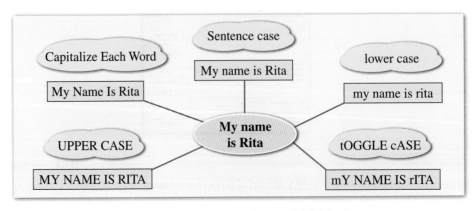

Text cases in MS Word 2010

How to change the case

Follow these steps to change the case of the text:
1. Select the text.
2. Click the drop-down arrow next to the **Change Case** option in the **Font** group of the **Home** tab.
3. Choose the required case for the selected text from the drop-down list. The case of the text will be changed.

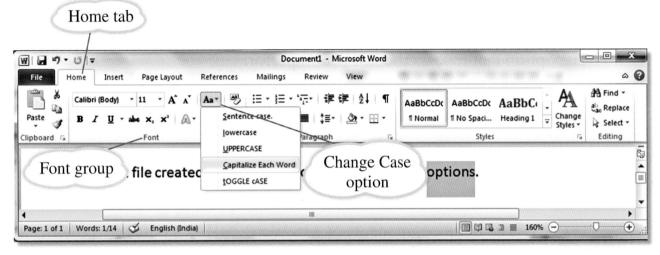

Changing the case of the text

ACTIVITY

Complete the following activity.
1. Make a document on MS Word called 'Myname.docx'.
2. Write a paragraph about yourself.
3. You might see that your name is highlighted as a spelling mistake as not all names are in the MS Word dictionary. Add your name to the Dictionary so that it doesn't show as an error in the next file.

GLOSSARY

Change Case The option that changes the case of the written text.

Copy The option that creates a duplicate (copy) of the selected text.

Cut The option that is used to move the selected text from one position to another.

Dialog box This is the small window that asks the user for some information/ gives information.

Find The option that searches a Word document for specified word(s).

Paste The option that places the Cut/Copy text at the required location.

Redo The option that repeats the last action performed.

Replace The option that changes the selected text to a new text.

Undo The option that reverses the last action performed.

YOU ARE HERE

3

1. The main components of MS Word 2010 window are the Title bar, Quick Access Toolbar, Ruler, Scroll bars, Work Area, Ribbon and Status bar.

2. You should select text when you wish to move it or make a copy of it.

3. Both the Cut and Copy options copy the text/object on to the Clipboard. To place it at the required position use the Paste option from the Home tab. This works in combination with either the Cut or the Copy options.

4. Specific words or a part of the text can be located in a document using the Find option. Text can also be replaced using the Replace option any number of times.

5. MS Word 2010 includes an automatic Spellchecker option. It is used for correcting spellings as they are typed. The Spelling & Grammar option in the Review tab helps the user change spelling and grammatical errors in the text.

6. To change the case of the written text, click on the Home tab ⟹ Font group ⟹ Change Case option.

EXERCISE

A. Give one word for the following.

1. It is used to change the length and width of a page. ....

2. It is the area in the document where you can type the text. ....

3. It contains some commonly used options like Undo, Redo and Save. ....

4. It is divided into tabs which are further divided into groups. ....

5. It provides information regarding page number, word count, language, page layout and zoom slider. ....

B. Match the following.

1. I am fond of reading books.   a. Toggle case

2. I Am Fond Of Reading Books.   b. Upper case

3. i AM FOND OF READING BOOKS.   c. Capitalize each word

4. i am fond of reading books.   d. Sentence case

5. I AM FOND OF READING BOOKS.   e. Lower case

C. Answer the following questions.

1. Explain the difference between the Cut and Copy options.
2. Name two scroll bars present on an MS Word 2010 window.
3. What is the purpose of the Find and Replace dialog box?
4. Name the editing tools on the Quick Access Toolbar.
5. Name all the options in the Change Case drop-down list.
6. What are the uses of the Spelling & Grammar tool?

D. Label the components of the MS Word 2010 window.

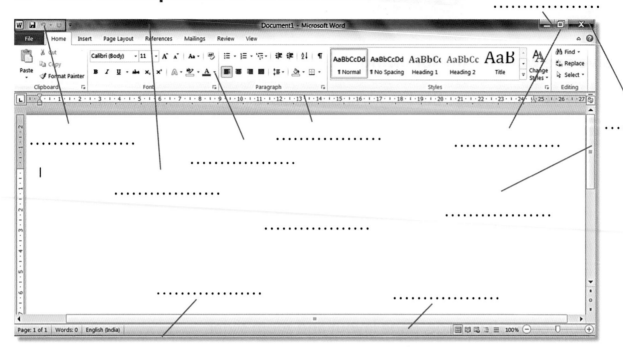

LAB WORK

Write step-by-step instructions for a beginner who is going to work on a MS Word document for the first time.

PROJECT WORK

Make a journal on how this week has been for you. Mention the new things you learnt in school this week. Say what you liked the most, what was interesting, which topics/skills you took some time learning and what did not work for you this week.

In MS Word 2016:

- Components of MS Word 2016 window are given below:

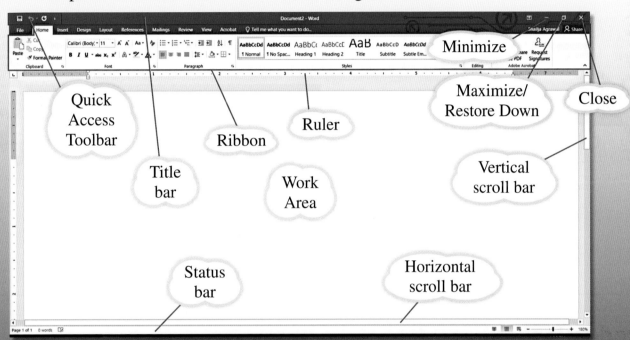

- In MS Word 2016, when you type an incorrect spelling, you see a red line below that word. To correct this, click on Spelling & Grammar option in the Review tab. Spelling & Grammar corrections appear on the right side of the window.

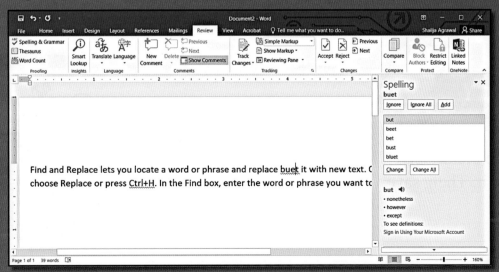

Using
Paint Tools

SNAP RECAP

1. What can you do using various components of Paint?

2. Discuss the functions performed by different tools in Paint.

LEARNING OBJECTIVES

You will learn about:

- working with Shapes: Curve tool, Polygon tool, Rounded rectangle tool
- how to fill shapes with color
- using tools in Paint: Select, Magnifier, Undo and Redo

Introduction

You have learnt about different Paint tools and shapes in your earlier classes. Now do the following activity to practise using these tools.

ACTIVITY

Create the picture given here using different Paint tools and color it. Then, save your file on the desktop.

Shapes

Let us learn about some more shapes in Paint.

Curve tool

The Curve tool is used to draw curves. Follow these steps to draw a curve.

1. Click on the **Curve** tool in the **Shapes** group of the **Home** tab.
2. Move the mouse pointer to the **Drawing Area**. Notice that the mouse pointer changes to a cross sign.
3. Left-click and drag the mouse to draw a line.
4. Click where you want the arc of the curve to be and then drag to adjust the curve.

Choose the color of the curve from the **Colors** palette in the **Home** tab.

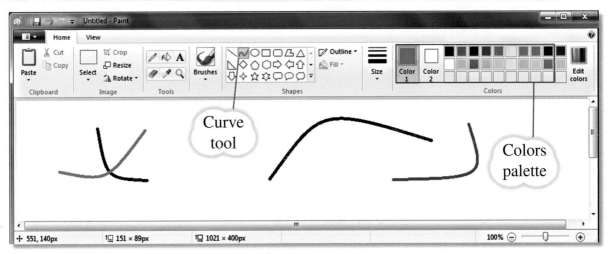

Using the Curve tool

Polygon tool

The Polygon tool is used to draw polygons. Polygons are shapes with three or more sides. Using this tool, you can only draw one side of the polygon at a time.

Follow these steps to draw a polygon.

1. Click on the **Polygon** tool in the **Shapes** group of the **Home** tab.
2. Move the mouse pointer to the **Drawing Area**. The mouse pointer changes to a cross sign.
3. Select the line color from the **Colors** palette. The default color is black.

4. Click where you want to start the polygon. Left-click and drag the mouse to form the first side of the polygon.

To draw smooth lines, press down and hold the Shift key while dragging the mouse button.

5. Start drawing from beside the point where you finished drawing the previous side.
6. Repeat the above step for the rest of the sides, except the last side.
7. To draw the last side, just double-click the left mouse button.

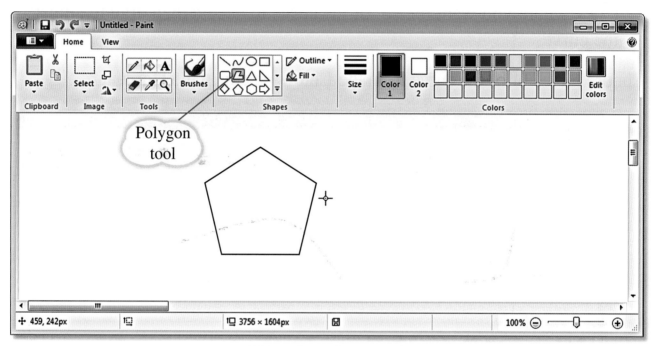

Using the Polygon tool

Rounded Rectangle tool ▭

The Rounded rectangle tool is used to draw rectangles with rounded corners.

Follow these steps to draw a rectangle with rounded corners.
1. Click on the **Rounded rectangle** tool in the **Shapes** group of the **Home** tab.
2. Select the line color from the **Colors** palette. Here, the line color is green.
3. Move the mouse pointer to the **Drawing Area**. The mouse pointer changes to a cross sign ⊹.

4. Left-click and drag the mouse to draw the rounded rectangle of desired size. The rectangle being drawn is seen alongside the mouse pointer.

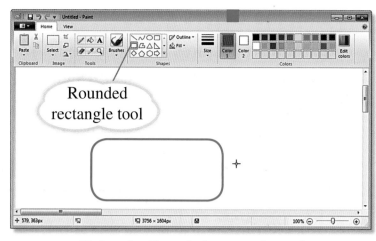

Rounded rectangle tool

Using the Rounded rectangle tool

How to fill color

You can color the shapes drawn in Paint using the following options.

Using the Colors group → Fill with color tool → Color picker tool

However, to be able to color the pictures drawn in Paint, you need to first understand the difference between closed and open figures. You also need to understand how to use options in the **Colors** group effectively.

Closed figure

Any figure that is closed from all sides without any gap is called a **closed figure**.

For example, a rectangle made using the Rectangle tool in the Shapes group is a closed figure. You can fill color in a closed figure as the color will not spill over onto the rest of the Drawing Area.

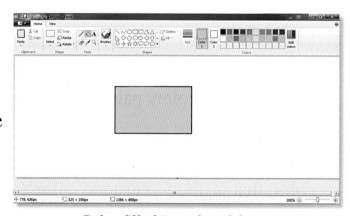

Color filled in a closed figure

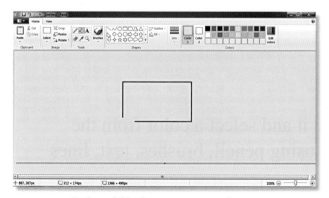

Color filled in an open figure

Open figure

Any figure that is open from any side or has a gap is called an **open figure**. If you draw a rectangle using the Pencil tool in the Tools group, there may be gaps between the lines. If you try to fill color in an open figure, the entire Drawing Area will be colored.

43

Using the Colors group

What fun are pictures without colors? To color the pictures you draw in Paint, use the colors given in the **Colors** group.

The **Edit Colors** option in the **Colors** group opens a palette of colors where you can make a new color from the available options.

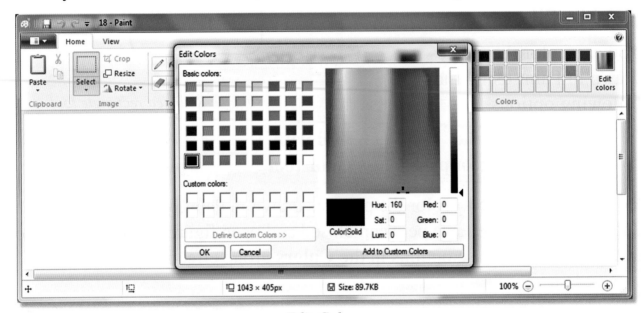

Edit Colors

New colors chosen or created using the **Edit Colors** option are added to the default 20 colors palette.

In the **Colors** group, you will notice two color boxes, **Color 1** and **Color 2**. Color 1 indicates the current color, that is, the foreground color and Color 2 is the background color.

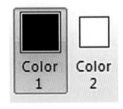

Colors boxes

You will now learn how to use the color boxes.

Color 1

To use the foreground color, left-click on it and select a color from the **Colors** group. This color is useful while using pencil, brushes, text, lines and borders of shapes.

Color 2 Color 2

To use the background color, left-click on it and select a color from the **Colors** palette. This color is used with eraser and for shape fills.

After selecting Color 1 and Color 2, you can draw colored images. To do so, follow the steps given below.

1. Click on **Color 1** and select a color of your choice from the **Colors** palette, say red.

2. Click on **Color 2** and select another color from the **Colors** palette, say yellow.

FACT FILE

Paint 3D is a free program from Microsoft that includes both basic and advanced art tools. Not only can you use brushes, shapes, text, and effects to create unique 2D art, but you can also build 3D objects and even remix models made by other Paint 3D users.

3. Select any closed shape from the **Shapes** group.

4. Bring the pointer to the **Drawing Area**.

5. Click and drag the mouse to draw the outline of the shape with the foreground color and fill the shape with the background color.

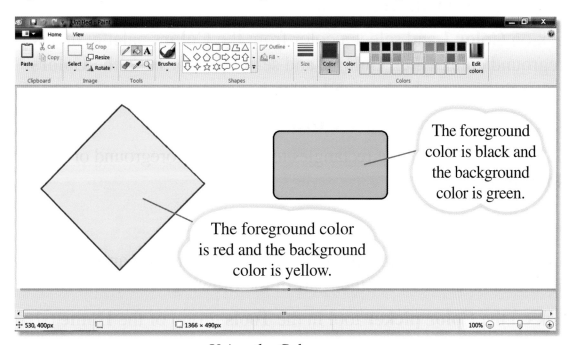

The foreground color is black and the background color is green.

The foreground color is red and the background color is yellow.

Using the Colors group

You can select a different medium for shape outline or shape fill by using the **Outline** and **Fill** options in the **Shapes** group, respectively.

Fill with Color tool

The **Fill with color** tool is used for filling color in a closed figure. Follow these steps to fill color in a closed figure:

1. Draw two closed figures, say rounded rectangles.

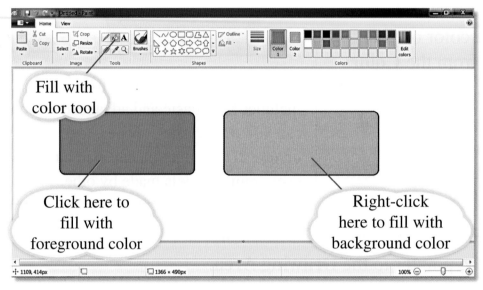

Using the Fill with color tool

2. Click on the **Fill with color** tool.

3. Click on **Color 1** and select a color from the **Colors** palette: this is your foreground color. Click **Color 2** and select a color from the **Colors** palette: this is your background color.

4. Move the mouse pointer to the **Drawing Area**.

5. Click or right-click on the rectangles to fill it with foreground or background color respectively.

Color Picker tool

The **Color picker** tool helps us to pick a color from one part of the drawing and fill the same color in another part of the drawing.

1. Click on the **Color picker** tool in the **Tools** group of the **Home** tab.

2. Click on the color in the picture which you want to pick. This color would be selected to fill in. Notice the color change in the **Color 1** box.

3. As soon as the color is selected, the **Color picker** tool icon changes to **Fill with color** tool icon.

4. Click on the desired area of the picture to fill it with the color picked.

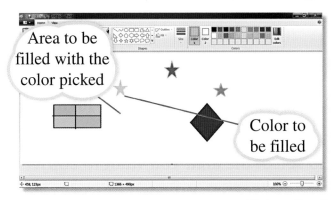 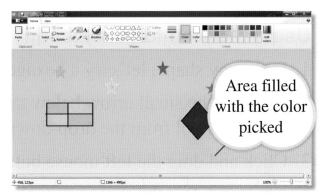

Using the Color picker tool

Brushes

The Brushes tool is used to draw lines that have a different appearance and texture – it is like using different artistic brushes. By using various brushes, you can draw free form and curved lines with different effects.

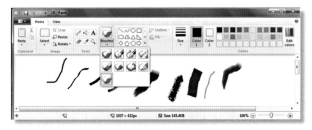

Brushes

More tools in Paint

Below are more examples of tools you can use in Paint.

Select

You can copy or move a part of a picture using the **Select** tool in the **Image** group of the **Home** tab. There are two kinds of selections that can be done.

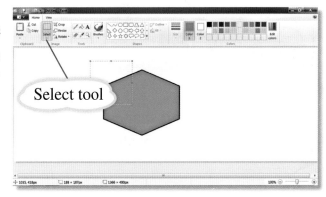

Using the Rectangular selection

1. Draw any shape, say a hexagon. Use the **Polygon** tool.

Using the Rectangular selection

2. Click on the **Select** tool. Notice that the mouse pointer changes to a cross .

3. Click and drag the mouse to select the rectangular area you want to move. A dotted rectangle now appears and the mouse pointer changes to a cross with four arrowheads.

4. Click and drag this selected portion of the hexagon to a new location.

Using the Free-form selection

1. Draw any shape, let's try a hexagon again. Use the **Polygon** tool.

2. Click on the small arrow below the **Select** tool icon. Select **Free-form selection** tool from the drop-down list.

3. Click and drag the left mouse button to select the area you want to copy.

4. Click and drag the dotted rectangle to a new location.

TRY THIS

Draw a picture in **Paint**.

Go to **Select**, choose the **Select all** ▢ option and move your whole picture to a new location.

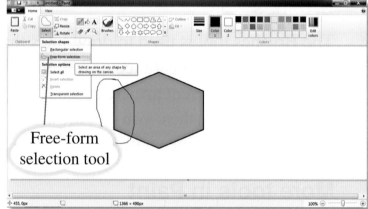

Free-form selection tool

Using Free-form selection

ACTIVITY

Draw a car using shapes of your choice. Select the shape using the appropriate selection tool and paste it in a new location on the Drawing Area.

Eraser tool

The Eraser tool is used for erasing any part of the drawing or the color filled in a figure. You can use this tool by clicking and dragging the mouse pointer over the area you wish to erase. You can increase or decrease the size of the eraser by using the options in the **Size** drop-down list.

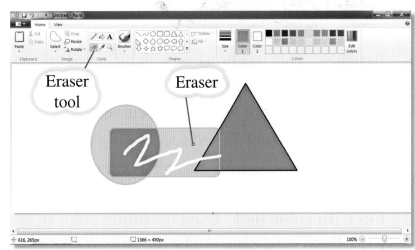

Erasing the drawing

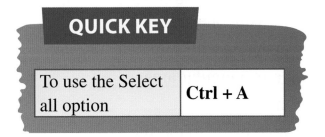

To use the Select all option	**Ctrl + A**

Magnifier tool

You may want to see a part of a drawing more closely. Using this tool you can zoom in or out of your drawing. To zoom in, just left-click on the part of the drawing you want to zoom into. To zoom out, right-click on the part of the drawing you want to zoom out of.

Undo and Redo

The Undo option allows you to undo the last action. It removes the last change you made to the file. While drawing a picture if you make a mistake, you can undo it by clicking on the **Undo** button on the **Quick Access Toolbar**.

You can redo or repeat the last action by clicking the **Redo** button from the **Quick Access Toolbar**.

QUICK KEY

To undo a change to the file	**Ctrl + Z**
To redo a change	**Ctrl + Y**

49

Brushes This has brushes with different appearances and texture that are used for drawing.

Curve tool Used for drawing curves.

Color picker tool Used for copying color from one figure to another.

Eraser tool Used for erasing a part of the drawing or the color filled in a closed figure.

Fill with color tool Used for filling color in closed figures.

Free-form selection Used for selecting an irregular area.

Magnifier tool Used for zooming in and out of the Drawing Area.

Polygon tool Used for drawing polygons by drawing one side at a time.

Rounded rectangle tool Used for drawing rectangles with rounded corners.

Rectangular selection tool Used for selecting a rectangular area.

Redo option This option repeats the last action.

Undo option This option removes the last change made to the file.

YOU ARE HERE

4

1. Closed figures have no gaps between the lines that form them.
2. Open figures have gaps in the lines that form them.
3. Foreground color is used for text, lines and borders of shapes.
4. Background color is used for coloring closed figures and the background of text boxes.
5. Select is used to copy and paste a part of the picture.
6. To remove the last change you made to the file, click on the Undo button in the Quick Access Toolbar. To repeat the last action, click on the Redo button.

EXERCISE

A. True or false? Correct the incorrect statements.

1. You can fill color in open figures.

   ....

2. The Redo option allows you to undo the last action.

   ....

3. To draw smooth lines press and hold the Ctrl key while dragging the mouse button.

   ....

4. New colors chosen or created using the Edit colors option are added to the default 20 color palette.

   ....

5. Using the Select tool you can zoom in or out of your drawing.

   ....

B. Name the following Paint tools.

1. [tool image]

   ....

2. [tool image]

   ....

3. [tool image]

   ....

4. [tool image]

   ....

5. [Select tool image]

   ....

C. Explain the difference between:

1. Open and closed figures
2. Foreground and background colors
3. Fill with color and color picker tools
4. Rectangular selection and free-form selection tools

51

D. Answer the following questions.

1. What is the Curve tool used for?

2. Which shapes can you draw using the Polygon tool?

3. Describe the different ways of filling color in a picture.

4. Explain how the Magnifier tool works.

5. Can you fill blue color in the following figures using the Fill with color tool in Paint? Yes or No? Explain your answer.

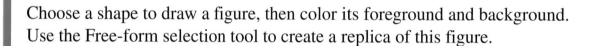

LAB WORK

Choose a shape to draw a figure, then color its foreground and background. Use the Free-form selection tool to create a replica of this figure.

PROJECT WORK

In the space given below, draw a figure of your choice using at least 5 shapes. Then, color the figure. Draw the same in Paint and save your drawing on the desktop.

Using the Text Tool in Paint

5

SNAP RECAP

Draw a 'Thank You' card for your teacher using different Paint tools.

LEARNING OBJECTIVES

You will learn about:
- the Text tool
- the Text tab
- components of the Text tab

Introduction

There may be times when you might like to include some text in your drawings.

For example, while making a birthday card for your friend in Paint you might want to write 'Happy Birthday'. In Paint, you can write the text using the Text tool.

Text tool A

The Text tool is used for inserting text in a picture.

Using the Text tool

1. Click on the **Text** tool in the **Tools** group of the **Home** tab.

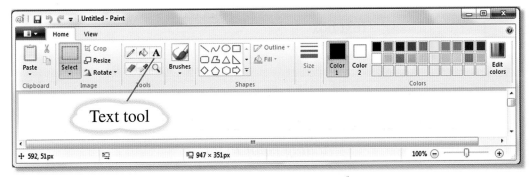

Text tool in the Home tab

2. Move the mouse pointer to the **Drawing Area**. Notice that the mouse pointer changes to an I shaped cursor.

3. Drag the mouse where you want to insert text. A dotted rectangle with a blinking cursor appears. The text you type will appear within this box. This box is called a **Text box**.

4. Type 'Text tool in Paint' using the keyboard.

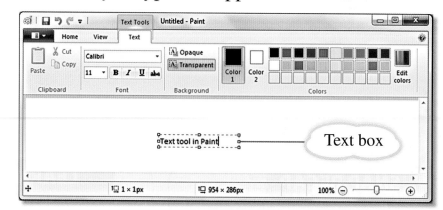

Using the Text tool

Typing text in color

1. Click on the **Text** tool in the **Tools** group of the **Home** tab.

2. Drag the cursor to draw a Text box in the **Drawing Area**.

3. Click on **Color 1**. Select color from the **Colors** palette of the **Text** tab – say, blue.

4. Move the mouse pointer to the **Drawing Area**.

5. Click inside the Text box to insert text. You can see a cursor inside the dotted box.

6. Type 'This text is blue' using the keyboard.

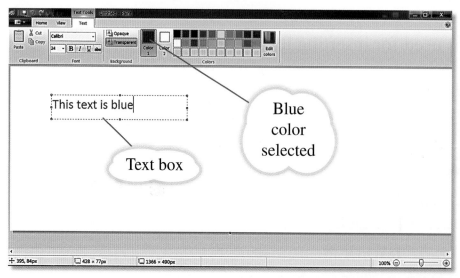

Adding color to text

54

Moving a Text box

You can move the Text box within the **Drawing Area**.

1. Move the mouse pointer to the boundary of the Text box.

2. When the mouse pointer changes to a cross with four arrowheads ✛, drag the Text box to a new location in the **Drawing Area**.

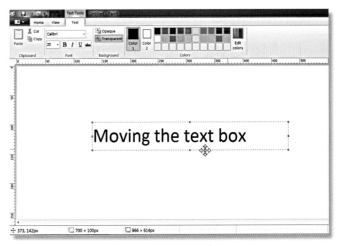

Moving a Text box

Changing the width of a Text box

You can resize the Text box to fit its text. Follow the steps given below:

1. With the Text box still selected, move the mouse pointer to the small square in the middle of the left or the right boundary of the Text box.

2. The mouse pointer changes to a double-headed arrow ⇔.

3. Drag the double-headed arrow away from the Text box to increase the width. Drag it inwards to decrease the width.

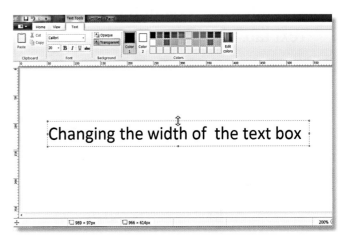

Changing the width of the Text box

Changing the height of the Text box

1. With the Text box still selected, move the mouse pointer to the small squares in the middle of the top or the bottom boundary of the Text box.

2. The mouse pointer changes to a double-headed arrow ↕.

3. Drag the double-headed arrow away from the Text box to increase the height. Drag it inwards to decrease the height.

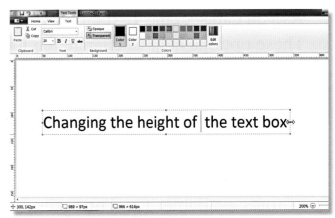

Changing the height of the Text box

Changing the width and height together

1. Move the mouse pointer to any of the four small squares at the corners of the Text box.

2. The mouse pointer changes to a double-headed arrow ⇔.

3. Drag the double-headed arrow away from the Text box to increase the size. Drag it inwards to decrease the size.

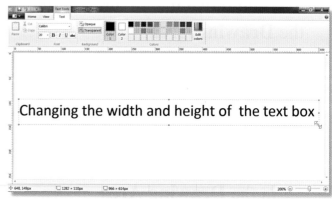

Changing the width and height together

Text tab

You have learnt to change the color of the text. But there are many other ways to change the look of the text in the Text box. These options are found in the Text tab.

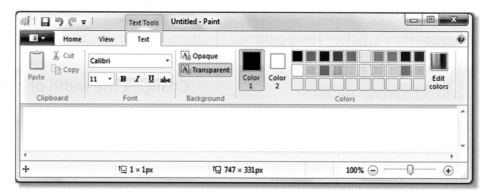

Text tab

The Text tab appears when you insert a Text box in the **Drawing Area**.

As you can see, the Text tab has a number of groups with different options. These options help us change the look of the text. They also help us adjust where the text is placed on the page. Making such changes to the text is called **formatting** the text.

Before you learn about the options in the Text tab, you should understand what a font is. Text can be written in a number of different styles. Each style is called a **font**. Every font has a name of its own. There are different types of fonts available. The **Font** group in the Text tab has options for changing the font and font size. Let us study them in detail.

Components of the Text Tab

Different components of the Text tab are shown below.

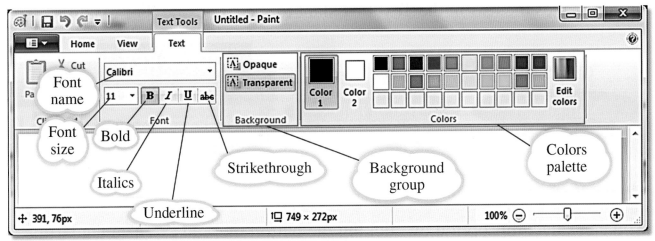

Components of the Text tab

Font name

The name of the font appears in the box on the left side of the Font group in the Text tab. Clicking on the arrow next to the box opens a drop-down list of fonts. You can select any one of the fonts in the list by simply clicking on the font name. A few popular fonts you are likely to see are Arial, Times New Roman and Calibri.

Font size

The font size appears in a box below the font name box. You can type in the font size you want by clicking on the box. You can also select the font size from a drop-down list by clicking on the arrow next to the box. An example of text in different font sizes is given here.

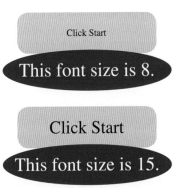

Bold

You can select this option by clicking the button marked **B**. The Bold option makes the text in the Text box darker than normal. This is called **boldface** text. For example,

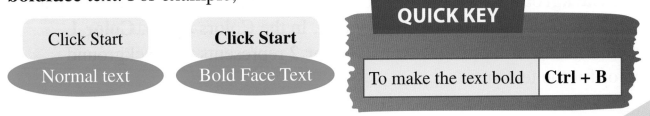

| To make the text bold | Ctrl + B |

QUICK KEY

Italic

You can select this option by clicking the button marked I. The Italic option makes the text in the Text box slant to the right side. For example,

QUICK KEY

| To make the text italic | Ctrl + I |

Underline

You can select this option by clicking the button marked $\underline{U}$. The Underline option underlines the text in the Text box. For example,

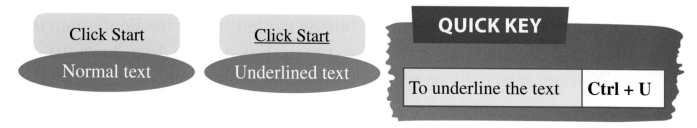

QUICK KEY

| To underline the text | Ctrl + U |

Strikethrough

You can select this option by clicking the button marked abc. The Strikethrough option strikes a line through the text in the Text box. For example,

Background group

The **Background** group allows you to fill the background of the text area using the Opaque or Transparent option. In the Colors group, **Color 1** represents the color of the text and **Color 2** represents the background color for the text area.

Opaque: This means the color given as background will hide everything beneath it.

Transparent: This means the color given as background will display everything beneath it, making it transparent.

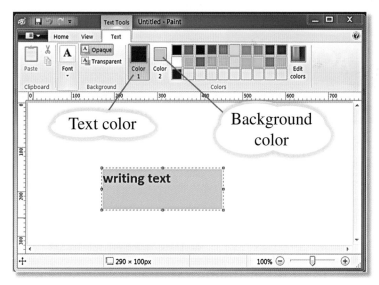

Background and color

Changing the background color of a Text box

Follow these steps to change the background color of the Text box.

1. Create a Text box.
2. Select **Color 2** and choose a color of your choice, say pink, from the **Colors** palette of the **Text** tab.
3. Select **Opaque** in the **Background** group.
4. Type the text.

TRY THIS

Repeat the same procedure once again, but this time select **Transparent** in the **Background** group instead of **Opaque** and type your text in the Text box.

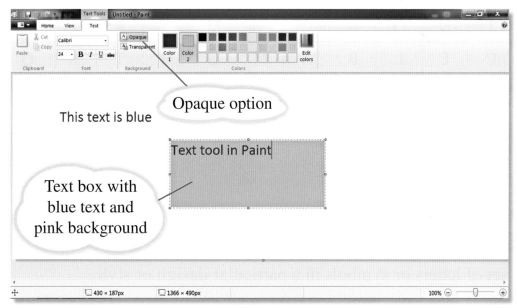

Changing the background

ACTIVITY

A. Give the formatting(s) applied to the following. One has been done for you.

1. *Bold* | Italics | 4. **Symbol** | |

2. <u>Italics</u> | | 5. *Font* | |

3. **Underline** | | 6. ***Format*** | |

B. Find the following words in the grid below.

| BOLD | COLOR | ITALIC | FORMAT | UNDERLINE |
| FONT | TOOLS | STRIKETHROUGH |

T	D	U	Y	T	P	L	C	O	L	O	R	P
O	F	N	N	Y	D	F	P	N	T	R	Y	K
O	H	D	B	G	B	O	L	D	R	T	P	L
L	I	E	V	V	G	N	Z	H	F	D	G	M
S	T	R	I	K	E	T	H	R	O	U	G	H
Z	A	L	C	S	S	W	W	L	R	S	D	F
C	L	I	S	Q	U	S	F	G	M	K	B	D
S	I	N	Q	W	C	V	M	J	A	L	N	C
W	C	E	L	B	N	M	G	H	T	K	Q	F

GLOSSARY

Bold   This option makes the text appear in boldface.

Font   A set of letters or symbols in a particular design or style.

60

Formatting   This is to apply a chosen appearance or style to text.

Italic   This makes the text slant to the right side.

Opaque   This means the colour chosen as the background will hide everything beneath it.

Strikethrough   This strikes a line through text.

Text box   This is the dotted rectangle in to which text is entered in Paint.

Transparent   This means the color beneath the background will be transparent, so you can still see all text beneath it.

Underline   This underlines the text.

YOU ARE HERE

5

1. You can change the color of the text and the background color of the Text box.

2. A Text box can be moved and resized.

3. The Text tab has options for changing the appearance of the text, its font and the font size.

4. No changes can be made to the text once you click outside the Text box.

EXERCISE

A.   Fill in the blanks.

1. In Paint, we write text using the ………. tool.

2. The Text tab appears when you insert a ……… . Box in the Drawing Area.

3. The ……………………….. option strikes a line through the text in the text box.

4. ……………………. applies a chosen appearance to text.

5. A set of letters or symbols in a particular design or style is called a …………. .

B. True or false?

1. The Text tool appears in the View tab.

2. The Text tool is used for inserting text in a picture.

3. You cannot change the background color of the Text box.

4. You can change both the width and height of the Text box together.

5. The Italic option makes the text in the Text box slant to the left side.

C. Name the following components of the Text tab.

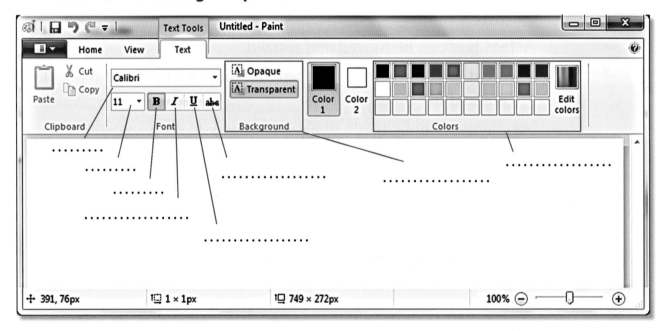

D. Answer the following questions.

1. How can you enter text in Paint?
2. What is a Text box?
3. Explain font name and font size. Give one example in each case.
4. How can you change the background color of a Text box?
5. Why do you need to be careful while working with Text boxes?

LAB WORK 🖥️

Make 3 different emojis/smileys and write down the emotion that each emoji represents.

Hello! How do you do?

PROJECT WORK

Design an information poster to share a message with others.

AN APPLE A DAY KEEPS THE DOCTOR AWAY!

Advanced Paint

SNAP RECAP

1. Open Paint and draw any picture using any five shapes. color and save the picture.

2. Identify the different tools used for drawing lines and shapes.

LEARNING OBJECTIVES

You will learn about:
- Home tab
- View tab

Introduction

You can draw and format pictures in Paint. You can also change the look and the orientation of the image created using different features of Paint. You will now explore these advanced features of Paint.

Editing images

In Paint, pictures can be edited using the **Cut**, **Copy** and **Paste** options available in the **Clipboard** group of the **Home** tab. You will now study them in detail.

Cut and Paste

To cut a part of the drawing in Paint, follow the steps given below:

1. Select a part of the drawing using the **Rectangular selection** or **Free-form selection** tool in the **Image** group of the **Home** tab.

2. Select the **Cut** option in the **Clipboard** group.

3. The part of the diagram selected is then stored in a temporary folder called **Clipboard**. You cannot view this. However, you can retrieve the diagram by selecting the **Paste** option.

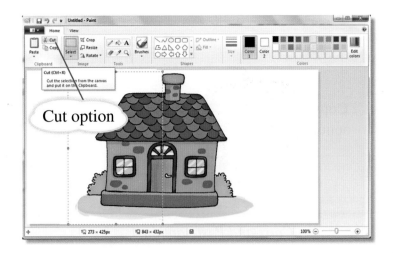

Selecting Cut option

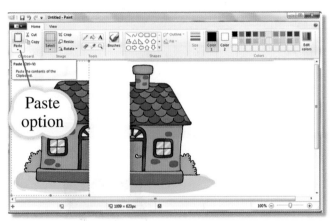

Using Paste option

4. Click the **Paste** option in the **Clipboard** group. The upper-left corner of the **Drawing Area** now displays the part of the diagram selected earlier.

QUICK KEY	
Cut selected part of the picture	**Ctrl + X**
Paste the cut part of the picture	**Ctrl + V**

Copy and Paste

To get a copy of the selected part of the picture in Paint, follow the steps given below:

1. Select the part of the drawing that needs to be copied.

2. Click the **Copy** and then the **Paste** option in the **Clipboard** group of the **Home** tab.

By copying the diagram, the original diagram remains as it is and does not change. Here also, the diagram selected is stored in the Clipboard.

3. The part of the diagram selected is copied at the upper-left corner of the **Drawing Area**.

4. The part of the diagram that has been pasted on the **Drawing Area** can also be shifted to a different place by clicking and dragging it.

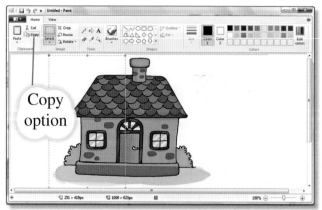

Copy and Paste options

Part of the picture copied and pasted

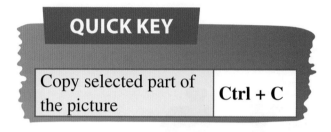

ACTIVITY

Draw a cat on Paint. Copy and paste it five times. Each time drag and shift the copied cat to a different location on the Drawing Area.

Image group

The **Image** group is used for changing the size of an image. Different options available in the Image group are Selection, Crop, Resize and Skew, and Rotate or Flip.

Select all

The **Select all** option is used for selecting all the objects that are included in the Drawing Area. You need to follow the steps given below:

1. Click **Select** drop-down list ⟹ **Select all** option in the **Image** group of the **Home** tab.

2. The entire **Drawing Area** will now be selected. You may now either **Cut** or **Copy** the selected area and **Paste** it onto a different file or a different document.

Select All option

Rotate or Flip

This option is used for flipping or rotating a part of or all the picture. To do so, follow these steps:

1. To rotate or flip the whole picture, click on the drop-down arrow next to the **Rotate** option in the **Image** group of the **Home** tab. Choose the direction of rotation or flip.

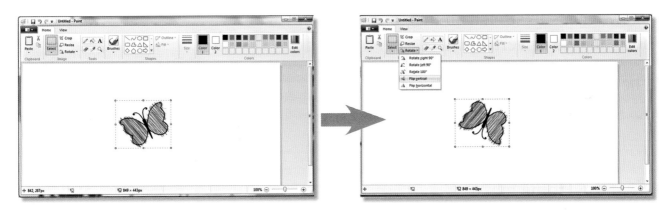

a. *Normal view*   **b.** *Vertical flipping*

Rotating or flipping the entire picture

2. To rotate or flip a part of a picture, click on **Select** in the **Image** group of the **Home** tab and select the particular part.

   Click the drop-down arrow next to **Rotate** and choose the direction of rotation or flip.

3. You can flip the picture horizontally or vertically. The picture can be rotated in different directions and at different angles.

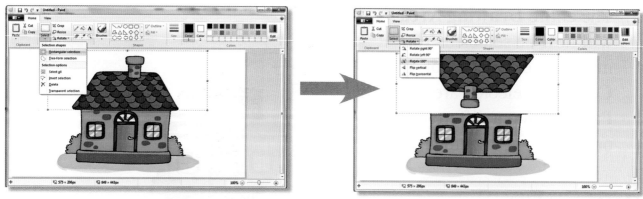

a. *Selecting a part of the picture*

b. *Rotating the selected part by 180°*

Rotating or flipping a part of the picture

Resize and Skew

You can use the Resize option to resize or skew the objects or a part of the object in a specific direction by an exact percentage or degrees.

Skew means to stretch an image horizontally or vertically.

The steps to use this option are:

1. Select the entire picture or part of the picture to be resized or skewed using the **Select** option in the **Image** group of the **Home** tab.

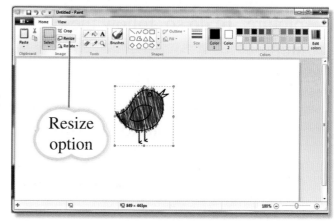

Selecting the entire picture for using the Resize and Skew option

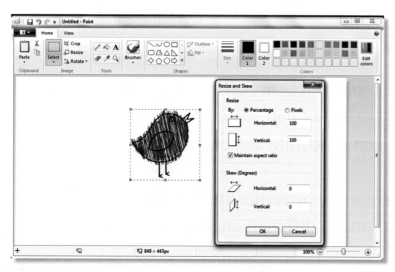

Resize and Skew dialog box

2. Click the **Resize** option in the **Image** group of the **Home** tab.

3. The **Resize and Skew** dialog box appears.

4. Ensure that the **Maintain Aspect Ratio** checkbox is selected.

68

5. In the **Resize** section, enter the new value for resizing the picture in either the **Horizontal** or **Vertical** box. The other will be filled in automatically if the **Maintain Aspect Ratio** checkbox is selected.

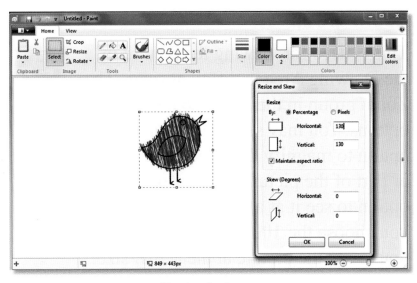

Resized picture

6. In the **Skew** section enter a value each in both the **Horizontal** and **Vertical** boxes.

7. Click **OK**. The picture will be both resized and skewed.

The **Resize** option resizes the picture, and the **Skew** option changes the angle of the picture.

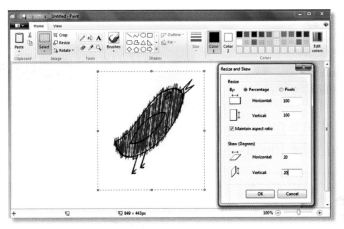

Skewed picture

View tab

The View tab is used to view the various options of Paint. The main options that can be selected in the View tab are shown here.

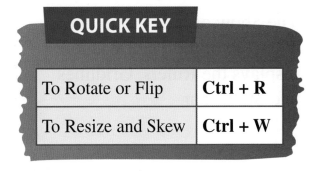

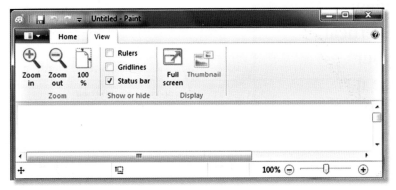

View tab

Zoom group

This is used for viewing the picture in the Drawing Area in different sizes. The Zoom group in the View tab has two options. You may select the **Zoom in** option to magnify the selected picture or part of the picture, or the **Zoom out** option to see it at a smaller size. When you choose the **100%** option, it allows you to see the picture at the actual size.

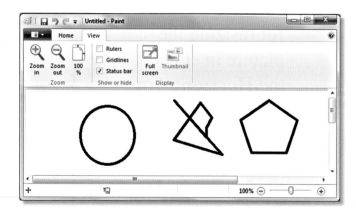

Zoom group

FACT FILE

You can also **Zoom in** (+) or **Zoom out** (−) in a picture using the slider at the bottom of the page in the lower-right corner of the Status Bar of the Paint window.

QUICK KEY

| Zoom in | **Ctrl + PgUp** |
| Zoom out | **Ctrl + PgDown** |

Show or hide group

The Show or hide group in the View tab of the Paint window displays the Rulers, Gridlines and Status bar.

Ruler

This helps you to view the horizontal and vertical measurements of your picture and to resize it.

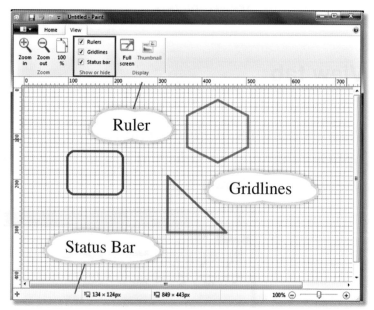

Show or hide group

Gridlines

This helps you to arrange your diagrams and pictures at appropriate locations in the Drawing Area of the Paint window. It also helps you to keep a track of the measurements of the picture.

Status bar

This helps you to keep track of the picture quality and zoom size of the Drawing Area.

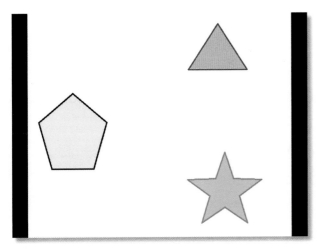

Full screen view

Display group

This option displays the picture either in full screen or as a thumbnail.

Full screen

This displays the drawing in the full screen mode. To exit from full screen mode, click anywhere on the screen and it takes you back to normal view.

Thumbnail

This allows you to see an enlarged picture in a small window within the drawing area.

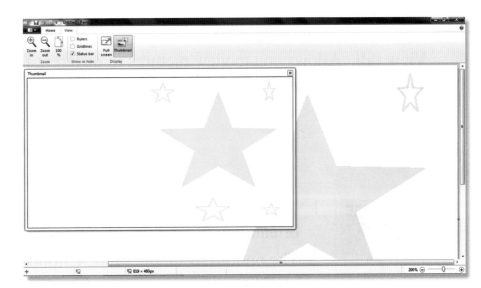

Thumbnail view

It's your friend's birthday. Using Paint, draw a card with triangles, circles and rectangles for the border. Add a birthday message for them. Use different features of Paint to make it attractive.

Happy Brithday

GLOSSARY

Clipboard   A temporary folder where the selected part of the picture is stored.

Full screen   Shows the Drawing Area in full screen mode.

Gridlines   Displays a graph-like grid in the Drawing Area.

Image group   Use this to change the size of an image.

Resize   This option resizes the image.

Select all   Use this to select the entire Drawing Area.

Skew   Changes the angle of the image.

Thumbnail   Displays the entire drawing in a small window in the Drawing Area.

View tab   Allows you to view pictures in different forms in Paint.

Zoom   Allows you to view pictures in different sizes in the Drawing Area.

YOU ARE HERE

6

1. The Home tab and View tab are used for changing the look and orientation of the picture created in Paint.

2. The options available in the Clipboard group are Cut, Copy and Paste.

3. The Image group includes the Resize, Rotate and Select options.

4. The options in the View tab include the Zoom, Show or hide and the Display group.

EXERCISE

A. Fill in the blanks with the correct word.

| Gridlines | Skew | Ctrl+PgUp | Ctrl+R | Thumbnail | Clipboard |

1. The .... command is used to see an enlarged picture in a small window.

2. .... helps you to arrange your diagrams and pictures at appropriate locations in the Drawing Area of the Paint window.

3. In Paint, pictures can be edited using the Cut, Copy and Paste options available in the .... group of the Home tab.

4. To rotate an image, ... is used.

5. To zoom in an image, ... is used.

6. .... changes the angle of the image.

B. Match the following.

1.	Cut, Copy and Paste		a.	Zoom group
2.	Rectangular selection		b.	Clipboard group
3.	Zoom in and zoom out		c.	Image group
4.	Ruler, Gridlines and Status bar		d.	Display group
5.	Full screen and Thumbnail		e.	Show or hide group

C. Give shortcuts for the following.

1. Cut   ....   2. Copy   ....

3. Paste   ....   4. Zoom out   ....

5. Rotate   ....   6. Resize   ....

D. Explain the difference between the following.

1. Cut and copy options
2. Zoom in and zoom out
3. Ruler and gridlines
4. Resize and skew
5. Full screen and thumbnail

LAB WORK

Make a logo for your school using a combination of shapes and drawing tools in Paint.

PROJECT WORK

A. Draw an identical pattern showcasing symmetry. An example is given here for your reference.

B. Draw a collage of a variety of leaves of different shapes and colors.

Tux Paint—Introduction

7

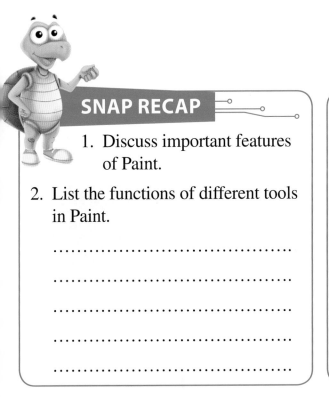

SNAP RECAP

1. Discuss important features of Paint.
2. List the functions of different tools in Paint.

   ....
   ....
   ....
   ....
   ....

LEARNING OBJECTIVES

You will learn about:
- features of Tux Paint
- starting Tux Paint
- components of the Tux Paint window
- drawing tools in Tux Paint
- saving a picture in Tux Paint
- opening a saved picture in Tux Paint
- erasing a saved picture in Tux Paint
- closing Tux Paint

Introduction

You already know how to draw and edit pictures using Paint. However, Paint is not the only application software that can be used for drawing and coloring. Tux Paint is a user-friendly application used for drawing and coloring purposes.

Features of Tux Paint

The Tux Paint drawing program is considered one of the best drawing programs due to the following features.

1. It is available for free and can be downloaded from the Internet.
2. It provides a large variety of tools that can be used while drawing. Special sound effects are heard when a tool is selected.

3. It provides a large variety of magical effects, special sound effects and animations that can be added to the drawing created by the user.

4. Its official mascot, the Linux Penguin, guides and helps the user understand different features of Tux Paint.

5. The images can be directly saved as thumbnails. You don't need to give a specific name to the file.

Starting Tux Paint

The Tux Paint software is freely available.

After the software is installed on your system, follow the steps given below:

1. Click on the **Start** button.

2. Select **All Programs** ⟹ **Tux Paint** ⟹ **Tux Paint (Full Screen)** to open it in full screen or **Tux Paint (Windowed)** to open it in a new window.

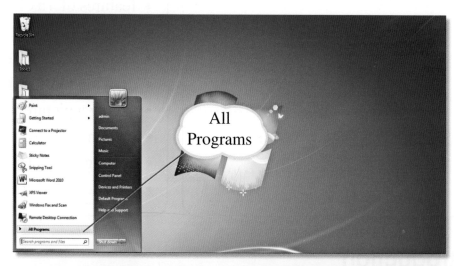

Opening Tux Paint

76

OR

Double-click the left mouse button on the **Tux Paint** desktop icon.

3. The **Tux Paint welcome** window opens.

The Tux Paint window is generally opened as a new window (**Windowed**) because all the options cannot be seen in the full screen.

Starting Tux Paint

Components of the Tux Paint Window

A standard Tux Paint window is shown below. The size of the Tux Paint window can be changed using the **Configure Tux Paint** tool.

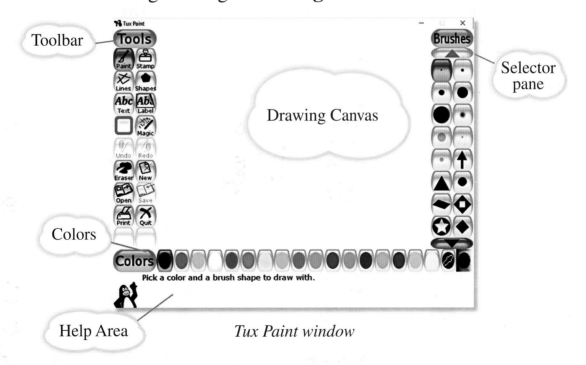

Tux Paint window

Toolbar

The different tools available in Tux Paint are seen in the left pane of the window. They are used for drawing, editing, saving and opening pictures.

Drawing Canvas

This is the blank area in the centre of the window used for creating images.

Selector pane

The right pane of the window shows the different options available under the tool selected in the Toolbar pane.

Colors

This is a palette of colors in the lower part of the Tux Paint window.

Help area

This area is represented by the Tux Paint mascot, Linux Penguin. It is found at the bottom of the Tux Paint window. Tips and information about the tool selected in the left pane can be seen here.

Drawing tools in Tux Paint

The different tools available in Tux Paint include Paint (Brushes), Stamp, Lines, Shapes, Text, Label, Magic, Undo, Redo and Eraser. Drawings can be saved, using other tools like Open, Save, Print and Quit. You can also open a new Drawing Canvas from here.

For every tool selected and used, a sound is heard in the background with the movement of the mouse.

Paint (Brushes)

This tool is used to draw freehand using the selected brush style and color.

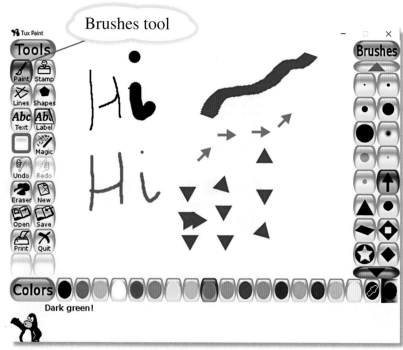

Using the Paint Brushes tool

Follow these steps to draw using the Paint tool:

1. Select the **Paint** tool in the **Toolbar** pane. The mouse pointer will change to the shape of a brush in the **Drawing Canvas**.

2. Select a color from the **Colors** palette.

3. Choose the size/thickness of the brush in the **Selector** pane.

4. Bring the mouse pointer to the **Drawing Canvas**, click on the left mouse button and drag it.

5. Release the mouse button after reaching the length you want.

Lines

This is used to draw straight lines.

Follow these steps to draw a line using the Line tool:

1. Click on the **Line** tool in the **Toolbar** pane. The mouse pointer will change to a cross in the **Drawing Canvas**.

2. Select a color from the **Colors** palette.

3. Select the size/thickness of the line in the **Selector** pane.

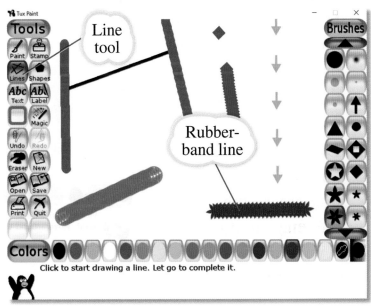

Using Line tool

4. Click on the left mouse button in the **Drawing Canvas** to mark the start of the line and drag the mouse.

As you drag the mouse, a thin rubber-band like line will be seen. It represents the area in the Drawing Canvas where the line will appear.

5. Release the mouse button when the line is the length you want.

Shapes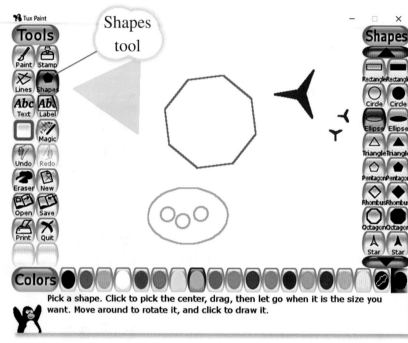

This is used to create simple, filled or unfilled shapes.

Follow these steps to draw a shape using the Shapes tool:

1. Click on the **Shapes** tool in the **Toolbar** pane. The mouse pointer will change to a cross in the **Drawing Canvas**.

2. Select a color from the **Colors** palette.

3. Click on your chosen shape in the **Selector** pane.

4. Bring the mouse to the **Drawing Canvas** and click the left mouse button to start drawing the shape from its centre.

5. Drag the mouse button further away to increase the size of the shape and release it when it is the size you want.

Using the Shapes tool

Move the left mouse button to rotate the shape in the direction you want and release the mouse button.

Text Abc

This tool is used to insert text and numbers in the picture.

Follow these steps to draw using the Text tool:

1. Click on the **Text** tool in the **Toolbar** pane. The mouse pointer will change to a I in the **Drawing Canvas**.

2. Select a color from the **Colors** palette.

3. Select a text style from the **Selector** pane.

The up and down arrows in the **Selector** pane can be used to make the font size bigger or smaller.

4. Bring the mouse pointer to the **Drawing Canvas** and click the left mouse button once. A blinking cursor will be seen. Type the text. Use the **Enter** key to move to the next line.

5. Click on your chosen location in the **Drawing Canvas** to move the text in the box to that location.

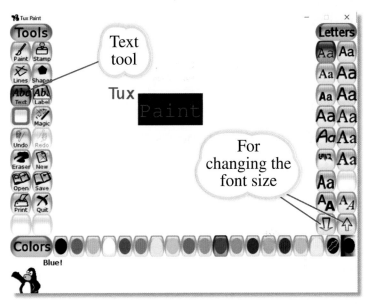

Using the Text tool

Magic

This is a set of tools with magical effects. These effects can be added to your drawings.

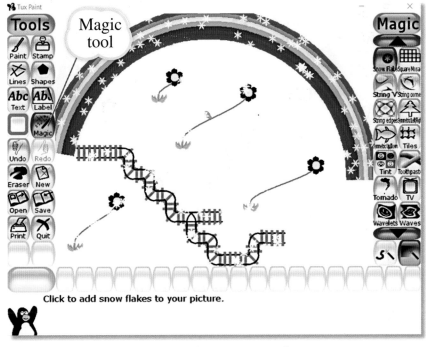

Using the Magic tool

Follow these steps to add effects using the Magic tool:

1. Click on the **Magic** tool in the **Toolbar** pane. The mouse pointer will change to a magic wand in the **Drawing Canvas**.

2. Select a magical effect from the **Selector** pane.

81

You can choose to apply a magical effect to specific parts of the picture by clicking the left mouse button at any locations you choose. You can also apply it to the entire picture by clicking and dragging. To do this, use the left and right arrow buttons below the down arrow in the **Selector** pane.

Undo and Redo

Pressing the **Undo** option cancels the last drawing action.

The **Redo** option repeats the last drawing action.

Both these options can be used more than once if there has not been a new drawing action.

Eraser

This is used to erase a part of the picture.

Follow these steps to erase a part of the picture using the Eraser tool:

1. Click on the **Eraser** tool in the **Toolbar** pane. The mouse pointer changes to a square with a plus sign in the centre.

2. You can select the size and shape of your eraser from the **Selector** pane.

3. Bring the mouse to your chosen location on the **Drawing Canvas**.

4. Hold the left mouse button and drag it to the part of the picture you want to erase.

5. Release the mouse button after the particular portion has been erased.

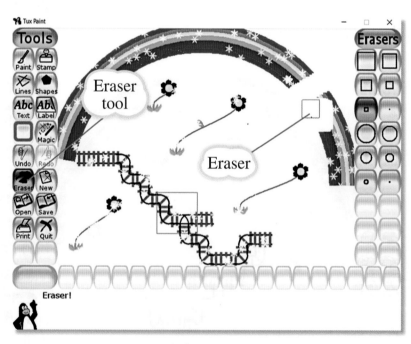

Using the Eraser tool

82

Saving a Picture

This tool is used to save the picture you are currently working on.

Click on the **Save** option in the **Toolbar** pane of the window to save your picture. It will be saved as a thumbnail in the virtual **Picturebook**.

If any further changes are made to the picture, then you need to save them. Follow the steps given below to do so.

1. Click on the **Save** option.

2. A dialog box will appear.

3. Click **Yes, replace the old one!** if you wish to save the picture over the older version, or click **No, save a new file!** for saving this picture as a new file.

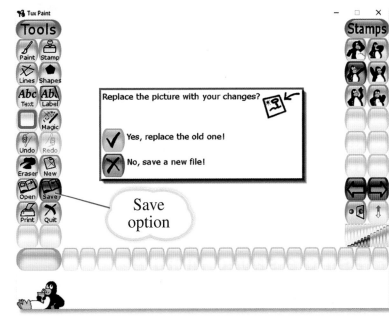

Saving a picture

ACTIVITY

Complete the following activity based on the instructions given.

1. Create a pattern using at least three shapes in Tux Paint.

2. Add four special effects to the image including one which is applied to the entire Drawing Canvas.

3. Give your picture an appropriate title using the font type and font style of your choice.

4. Save your picture in the virtual picturebook.

Opening a saved picture

This tool is used to open a picture saved in the virtual Picturebook.

Follow these steps to open a saved picture:

1. Click the **Open** option in the **Toolbar** pane. The virtual **Picturebook** window will appear.

2. Select the saved image from the list of options.

3. Click on the **Open** option near the lower-left part of the window, or click on the **Back** option to go back to the Tux Paint drawing window.

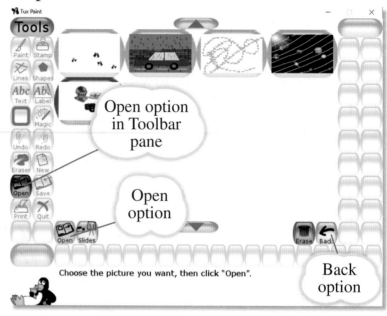

Opening a saved picture

Erasing a saved picture

You can also remove a saved picture from the virtual Picturebook.

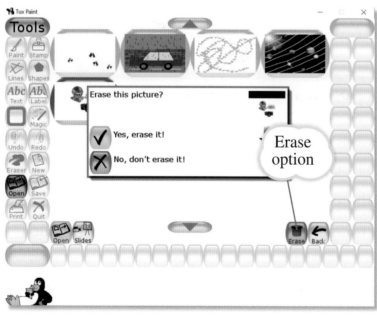

Erasing a saved picture

Follow these steps to remove a saved picture:

1. Open the virtual **Picturebook** using the **Open** option.

2. Select the picture to be removed.

3. Click on the **Erase** option.

4. A dialog box will appear.

5. Click **Yes, erase it!** if you wish to erase the picture from the virtual Picturebook, or else click **No, don't erase it!**

Closing Tux Paint

Follow these steps to close Tux Paint.

1. Click on **Quit** option in the **Tux Paint** window.

2. A dialog box will appear.

TRY THIS

Go to the picturebook and click on **Slides**. Press **Play** to view a slideshow of all the saved pictures in the virtual Picturebook.

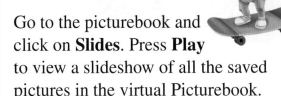

Quit dialog box

3. Click on **Yes, I'm done!** if you wish to close Tux Paint, or click **No, take me back!** to continue working.

4. If changes made to the picture have not been saved, a new dialog box will appear. It will ask you to either save the changes or discard them. Click **Yes, save it!** option to save the changes or click the **No, don't bother saving!** option.

QUICK KEY

To quit Tux Paint window	**Esc key**

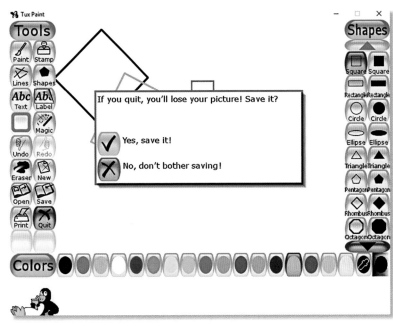

Save or discard changes dialog box

ACTIVITY

Complete the following activity.

1. Create a landscape picture in Tux Paint using the tools of your choice. Use at least five magical effects.

2. Save this picture in the virtual Picturebook as 'My Drawing'.

3. Open the Picturebook and open the picture you created in the previous activity. Draw lines to make a border for the picture.

4. Save the changes you have made to the picture as a new file.

5. Close the application software.

GLOSSARY

Colors   The color palette that can be used to create pictures in Tux Paint.

Drawing Canvas   The drawing space in the Tux Paint window.

Help Area   The area at the bottom of Tux Paint window where important tips and information regarding the selected tool is given by the Linux Penguin.

Selector pane   The pane on the right of the Tux Paint window. It contains the different options available for the tool selected in the Toolbar pane.

Tux Paint   A free drawing software for children.

Toolbar pane   The pane on the left of the Tux Paint window, which contains all the tools available for use.

1. Tux Paint provides a large variety of easy-to-use tools.

2. A sound is heard in the background when a tool is selected or a drawing step is completed by the user.

3. Tux Paint has tools like Paint (Brushes), Lines, Shapes, Text, Label, Eraser, Save, Open, Undo, Redo, Print and Quit. It has a Magic tool that can be used to add magical effects to a picture.

4. Pictures are saved as thumbnails in the virtual Picturebook. These images can be re-opened and modified. New files can be saved over the older versions or saved as new files.

5. Pictures can be erased from the virtual Picturebook.

EXERCISE

A. Give one word for the following.

1. This tool is used to draw straight lines. ....

2. This tool is used to insert text and numbers in the picture. ....

3. This is a set of tools with magical effects. ....

4. This option repeats the last drawing action. ....

5. The drawing space in the Tux Paint window. ....

B. Fill in the blanks using the correct word from the help box.

Undo	Selector	Text	Linux Penguin
	Picturebook	Configure Tux Paint	

1. The official mascot of Tux Paint is the ....

2. The .... tool can be used to change the size of the Tux Paint window.

3. The up and down arrows in the .... pane can be used to increase or decrease the font size.

4. Pressing the .... option cancels the last drawing action.

5. The pictures are saved as thumbnails in the virtual ....

6. .... tool is used to insert text and numbers in the picture.

C. Label the main screen of Tux Paint.

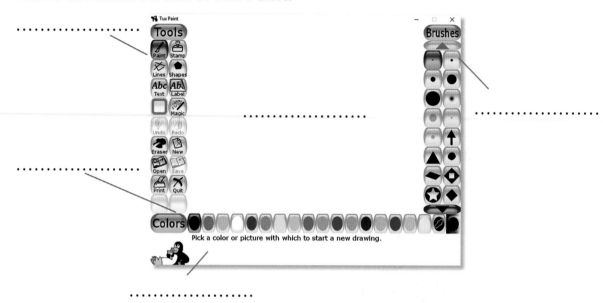

D. Match the following.

1. Close application   a. Brushes

2. Tux mascot   b. Thumbnails

3. Toolbar   c. Quit option

4. Paint   d. Linux Penguin

5. Picturebook   e. Left window pane

E. Answer the following questions.

1. Explain the differences between Paint and Tux Paint.

2. What are the components of the Tux Paint window?

3. Write the steps to draw a rectangle in Tux Paint using the Line tool.

4. Why is it better to open Tux Paint in a new window?

5. List the steps to erase a saved picture in Tux Paint.

6. Describe how the shape of the pointer changes on bringing it to the Drawing Canvas after choosing the different tools.

Using Tux Paint software, do the following:

A. Make a colorful picture of a party. [*Hint:* you could show balloons, cake, children enjoying the party, etc.]

B. Design a colorful bed cover or curtain for your room by creating patterns using different shapes.

PROJECT WORK

Draw a colorful scene on the theme 'Rainy Day' using Tux Paint.

Hint: Here is a sample drawing in Tux Paint.

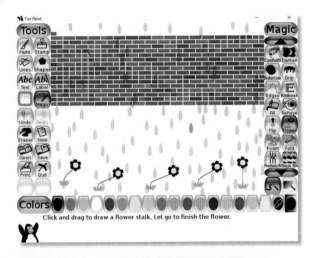

WHO AM I?

I am one of the developers of an open source drawing software program called Tux Paint.

In 2007, I received the MacBreak Weekly "Pick of the Week" award for Tux Paint.

I have also developed a wide range of open source games for various platforms.

I am ....

MSWLogo— Introduction

Introduction

A computer does not understand any of the languages you speak. You have to instruct a computer in a language it understands. These instructions are called **commands**. Logo is one of the languages that a computer understands.

LEARNING OBJECTIVES

You will learn about:

- starting MSWLogo
- the MSWLogo window
- the MSWLogo screen and its components
- the Commander window and its components
- exiting MSWLogo

Logo is a simple computer language. It can be used for drawing figures and designs, typing text and performing calculations.

Starting MSWLogo

The version of Logo used in Microsoft Windows is called **MSWLogo**. The steps to start MSWLogo are:

1. Click on the **Start** button.
2. Select **All Programs**.

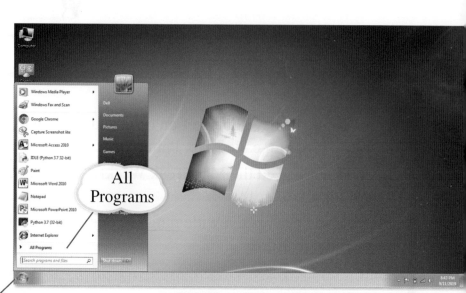

Selecting All Programs

3. Select the **Microsoft Windows Logo** folder.
4. Click on the **Microsoft Windows Logo** option.

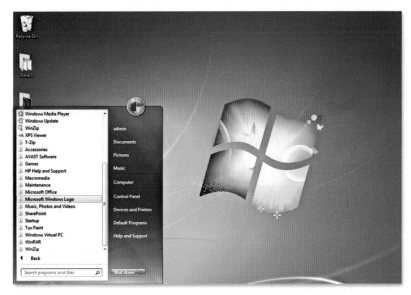

Selecting Microsoft Windows Logo option

MSWLogo window

The window of MSWLogo appears as one but is actually two separate windows. The upper window is the **MSWLogo screen** and the lower window is the **Commander** window. You can resize both these windows.

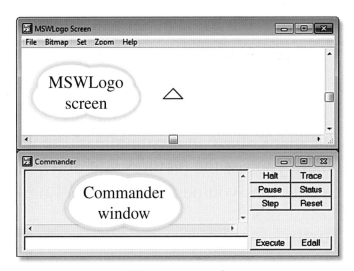

MSWLogo window

Components of the MSWLogo screen

The components of the MSWLogo screen are shown below.

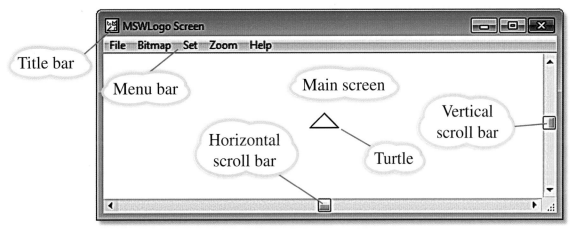

MSWLogo screen

You will now learn more about these components.

Title bar

The **Title bar** shows the name of the software 'MSWLogo Screen'. It also has the Minimize, Maximize/Restore Down and Close buttons. Minimizing or closing the MSWLogo screen also minimizes or closes the Commander window.

Title bar

Menu bar

The **Menu bar** lists the commands that MSWLogo can carry out. These are sorted into different menus. MSWLogo has the basic File and Help menus. It also has the Bitmap, Set and Zoom menus.

Menu bar

Main screen

The blank space in the middle of the window is the **Main screen**. It is where you see the pictures you draw, the text you type and the result of the calculations you perform in MSWLogo.

Turtle

The small triangle you see in the middle of the Main screen is called the **Turtle**. You can give instructions or commands to the turtle to move. When the turtle moves, it leaves a line behind. The Turtle is called the pen, as it draws for you.

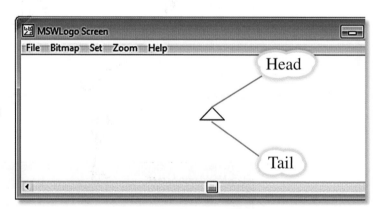

Parts of the turtle

You can tell the turtle how many steps to take and in which direction. This is how you draw figures using MSWLogo.

The turtle has two parts. The top of the turtle is known as the **head**. The head of the turtle shows the direction it is facing. The bottom of the turtle is known as the **tail**.

Scroll bars

There are scroll bars below and to the right of the Main screen. You can move up and down the Main screen using the scroll bar on the right. The scroll bar at the bottom allows you to move horizontally on the Main screen.

ACTIVITY

Find the following words in the grid below.

| MSWLOGO | SET | FILE | BITMAP | ZOOM |
| TURTLE | | HEAD | TAIL | |

Q	F	X	F	X	T	A	I	L
W	I	B	D	W	U	N	R	T
X	L	I	S	T	R	B	L	Y
S	E	T	C	L	T	W	Q	Z
B	V	M	S	W	L	O	G	O
N	C	A	M	H	E	A	D	O
M	G	P	H	J	L	J	R	M

FACT FILE

When Logo was being created, commands to move were given to a round-shaped robot. This robot would then roll around on the floor. This is why the robot came to be known as the turtle. Later, the robot was replaced with the triangle you see on the screen. But it is still called a turtle!

Components of the Commander window

The different components of the Commander window are shown below.

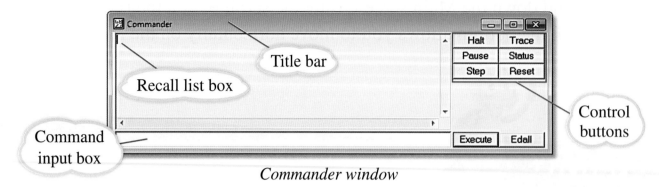

Commander window

Title bar

The Title bar of the Commander window has Minimize, Maximize/Restore Down and Close buttons. Minimizing the Commander window reduces it to a button on the taskbar of the desktop. When the Commander window is maximized, it covers the MSWLogo screen completely. The Commander window cannot be closed on its own. When you close the MSWLogo screen, it also closes the Commander window.

Title bar

Recall list box

The grey box below the Title bar is the Recall list box. It lists all the commands you give to Logo. If something goes wrong, a message is shown in this box. It is also where you see the text and the results of the arithmetic calculations that Logo performs.

Recall list box

Command input box

The box below the Recall list box is called the Command input box. This is where you type in commands.

```
FD 100|
```

Command input box

Control buttons

The buttons on the right side of the Recall list box are called **Control buttons**. These buttons are used to perform different tasks. You will now learn about some of them in detail.

Halt	Trace
Pause	Status
Step	Reset
Execute	Edall

Control buttons

TRY THIS

Press the **Enter key** to execute commands.

Halt button

This immediately stops Logo from carrying out the last command that was given.

Trace button

You may make mistakes while giving commands to Logo. The Trace button helps you find these mistakes. Removing such mistakes is called **debugging**.

Pause button

This stops Logo from carrying out a command temporarily. You can check the command you have entered and make corrections. After you have made the necessary corrections, you can click the Continue button or the Cancel button.

Status button

This opens the Status window which shows the current settings in Logo. When you click it once, the name of the button changes to NoStatus. Click the NoStatus button to close the Status window.

Reset button

This button clears the Main screen and places the turtle back in the centre of the screen.

Execute button

This button makes Logo carry out the command entered in the Command input box. The process is called **executing** or **running** a command.

Exiting MSWLogo

Follow these steps to exit Logo:

1. Click on **File** menu.
2. Click on **Exit**.

1. Type 'Bye' in the Input box.
2. Press the **Enter** key on the keyboard or click the **Execute** button in the Commander window.

1. Click the Close button in the Title bar.

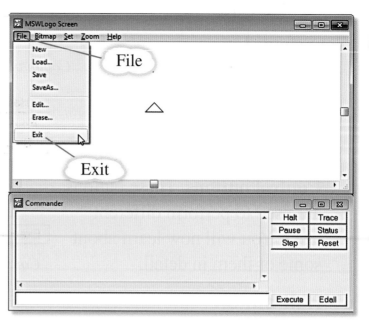

Exiting Logo using File menu

Command input box   The box where the commands are typed.

Debugging   The process of removing mistakes from the commands given.

Execute button   This makes MSWLogo carry out a command.

Halt button   This immediately stops MSWLogo from carrying out the last command given.

Main screen   The blank screen in the middle of the window.

Menu bar   This lists the commands that MSWLogo can carry out.

MSWLogo   A version of Logo used in Microsoft Windows.

Pause button   This stops MSWLogo from carrying out a command temporarily.

Recall list box   This lists the commands you give to MSWLogo.

Reset button   This clears the Main screen and places the turtle in the centre of the screen.

Status button   This opens the Status window.

Title bar   This shows the name of the software.

Turtle   The small triangle seen in the middle of the Main screen. It is the pen of Logo.

Trace button   This helps to find mistakes in the commands given.

1. MSWLogo is a simple computer language that can be used for drawing figures and designs, typing text and doing calculations.

2. The MSWLogo window has two parts – MSWLogo screen and Commander window.

3. The Title bar, Menu bar, Main screen, Turtle and Scroll bars are parts of the MSWLogo screen.

4. The MSWLogo turtle has a head and a tail. It is used to draw.

5. The Title bar, Recall list box, Command input box and Control buttons are parts of the Commander window.

6. The Recall list box shows the result of calculations. It also shows an error message when something goes wrong.

7. The various Control buttons are Halt, Trace, Pause, Status, Step and Reset.

EXERCISE

A. True or false?

1. The small triangle you see in the middle of the Main screen is called the turtle.

2. The turtle has three parts.

3. The box above the Recall list box is called the Command input box.

4. The Halt button immediately stops Logo from carrying out the last command that was given.

5. Debugging is the process of removing mistakes from the commands given.

97

B. Solve the crossword using the clues given.

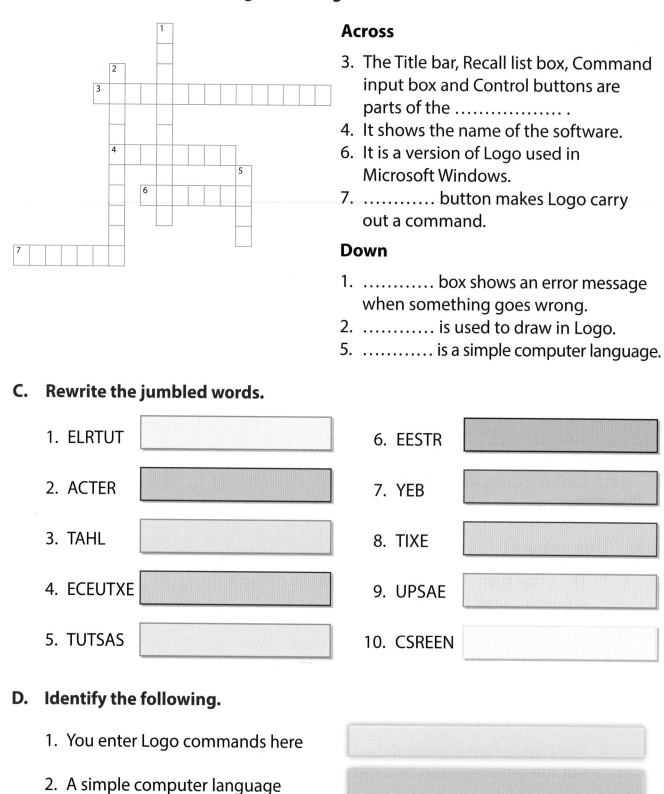

Across

3. The Title bar, Recall list box, Command input box and Control buttons are parts of the ....
4. It shows the name of the software.
6. It is a version of Logo used in Microsoft Windows.
7. .... button makes Logo carry out a command.

Down

1. .... box shows an error message when something goes wrong.
2. .... is used to draw in Logo.
5. .... is a simple computer language.

C. Rewrite the jumbled words.

1. ELRTUT
2. ACTER
3. TAHL
4. ECEUTXE
5. TUTSAS

6. EESTR
7. YEB
8. TIXE
9. UPSAE
10. CSREEN

D. Identify the following.

1. You enter Logo commands here

2. A simple computer language

3. The small triangle used to draw in Logo

4. Makes Logo carry out a command

5. Shows the direction turtle is facing

E. Answer the following questions.

1. What is MSWLogo?
2. What are the steps for starting MSWLogo?
3. What is a turtle in Logo?
4. What are the different components of the MSWLogo Commander window?
5. Can you use the Halt button to stop Logo from carrying out a command temporarily? Give reasons.

LAB WORK 🖵

A. Open the MSWLogo software on your computer. Observe how many Control buttons there are in the Commander window. Draw these buttons in Paint. Also using the Text tool, write the functions of the Execute and Halt buttons.

B. Practise opening and exiting the MSWLogo screen.

C. Using Paint, draw a turtle of different colors, shapes and sizes.

PROJECT WORK

In your computer lab, check the MSWLogo screen and list the different options available in all the menus in the Menu bar.

You could type the list in Microsoft Word.

MSWLogo— Basic Commands

9

SNAP RECAP

1. What are the steps for starting MSWLogo?
2. Discuss the functions of components of MSWLogo.

LEARNING OBJECTIVES

You will learn about:
- FORWARD command
- BACKWARD command
- RIGHT command
- LEFT command
- HOME command
- SETH command
- CLEARSCREEN command
- CLEARTEXT command
- HIDE TURTLE command
- SHOW TURTLE command
- REPEAT command
- BYE command

Introduction

As you have already learnt, the instructions that you give to a computer are called **commands**. In the case of Logo, these instructions are given through some specific **keywords**. Logo understands only these keywords. Each of these keywords tell the turtle in Logo to perform special kinds of task. These commands are called **primitives**. They are called primitives as they are very simple to remember. You will learn to use some basic commands.

When you first start Logo, the turtle is always in the centre of the Main screen. This is the turtle's **HOME** position. You can move the turtle from this HOME position by giving some commands. As the turtle moves, it leaves a line behind. This is how you draw figures and designs in Logo.

Forward command (FD)

This command is used for moving the turtle forward, in the direction it is facing, by a specified number of steps. The turtle also needs to know how far it should move. So along with the FORWARD command, you should also tell the turtle how many steps it should move in the forward direction. The short form for the FORWARD command is FD.

Using the FORWARD command

Follow these steps to use the FORWARD command:

1. Move the mouse pointer to the Input box. Note that the mouse pointer now changes to a cursor.

2. Click the Input box. A flashing bar appears. This means you can now type the command.

3. Type **FORWARD** or **FD**.

4. Press the **Space Bar** key.

5. Type the number of steps, for example, 100.

6. Click on the **Execute** button or press the **Enter** key.

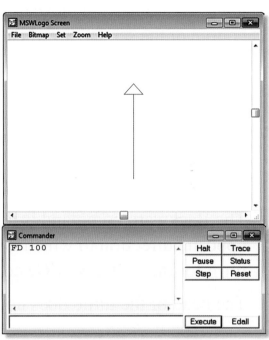

Forward command

The turtle moves forward by 100 steps in the direction in which its head is pointing. But how does the turtle measure steps?

You see the Main screen as a blank area. But for Logo, the Main screen is divided into rows and columns. Two horizontal lines make a **row** and two vertical lines make a **column**. Where a row and a column meet, they make a **square**. All these rows and columns together make a grid of squares. It is through this grid that Logo measures the steps that the turtle takes.

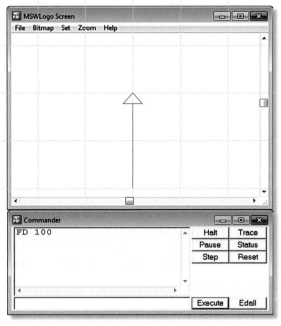

Logo grid of squares

The space in the Main screen is fixed. What happens if you tell Logo to move the turtle a long distance with a command such as FD 800? In this case, the turtle will first move to the very top of the screen. Then, since it cannot move forward any more, it will go around and move up from the bottom of the screen. So whenever you command Logo to move the turtle further than the space available on the screen, the turtle comes around the opposite side. In other words, it wraps around the screen.

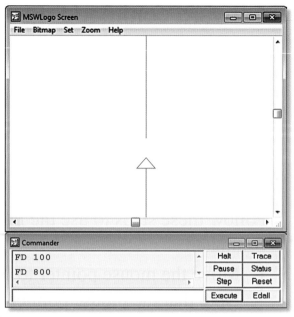

The turtle wraps around the LOGO screen

BACKWARD command (BK)

The Backward command is used for moving the turtle backward, in the opposite direction to which it is facing, by the specified distance. The short form for the BACKWARD command is BK.

The head of the turtle does not change.

Using the BACKWARD command

To draw a line in the backward direction:
1. Type **BACKWARD** or **BK**.
2. Press the **Space Bar** key.
3. Type the number of steps. For example, 100.
4. Press the **Enter** key or click on the **Execute** button.

You can even move the turtle forward with the BACKWARD command. You can do this by giving a negative number as the number of steps. For example, BK −100 will move the turtle forward by 100 steps.

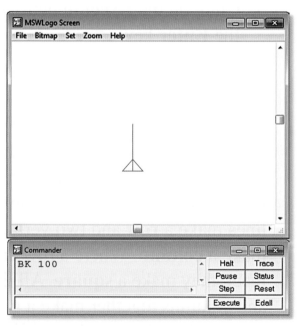

Using the BACKWARD command

You can move the turtle backwards using the FORWARD command. For example, FD −100 will move the turtle backwards by 100 steps.

RIGHT command (RT)

The RIGHT command turns the head of the turtle towards the right side, that is, in the clockwise direction. Though the turtle rotates, it stays in the same position. The short form for the RIGHT command is RT.

Using the RIGHT command

Follow these steps to move the turtle to the right:

1. Type **RIGHT** or **RT**.
2. Press the **Space Bar** key.
3. Type any number. For example, 90.
4. Press the **Enter** key.

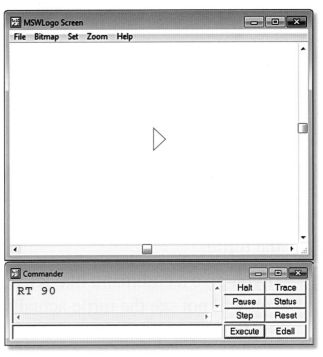

Using the RIGHT command

LEFT command (LT)

The LEFT command turns the head of the turtle towards the left side, that is, in the anti-clockwise direction. Though the turtle rotates, it stays in the same position. The short form for the LEFT command is LT.

Using the LEFT command

Follow these steps to move the turtle in the left direction:

1. Type **LEFT** or **LT**.
2. Press the **Space Bar** key.
3. Type any number. For example, 90.
4. Press the **Enter** key.

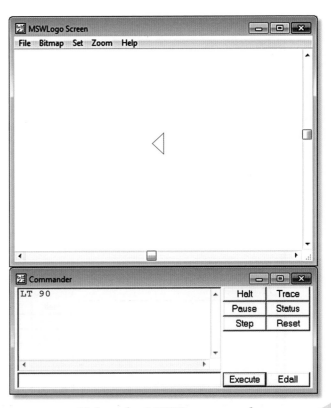

Using the LEFT command

Turtle making a circle   *Spinning on the ball of your foot*

In this example, the number 90 tells Logo how much it should turn the turtle.

Logo rotates the turtle in a circle. It is just like spinning on the ball of your foot while dancing.

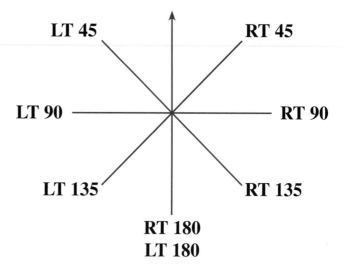

Rotating the turtle

The figure on the right will help you understand the commands that are used to rotate the turtle.

If you give a command like RT 360, you will not see the turtle actually rotate. This is because the turtle would have completed one turn and come back to its original position.

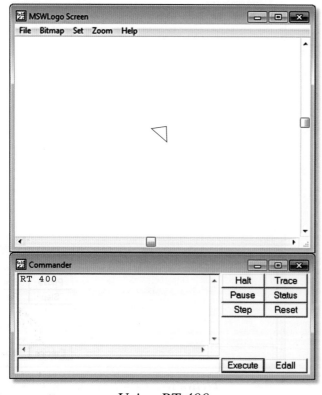

Using RT 400

What if the number typed is more than 360? In such a case, the turtle would first complete one turn and then start a new circle but at the same position. For example, if you give a command like RT 400, you will see the turtle rotating only by 40. This is because 400 – 360 is 40.

ACTIVITY

Draw a square in MSWLogo using the commands given below. Logo allows you to give more than one command. You could type all the commands for drawing a square and then press the Enter key. Try it!

FD 100 RT 90 FD 100 RT 90 FD 100 RT 90 FD 100 RT 90

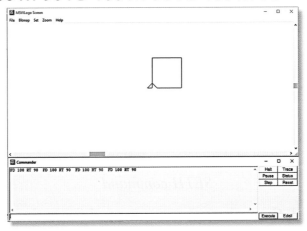

HOME command

The HOME command brings the turtle back to its starting position. The starting position of the turtle is the centre of the Main screen with its head pointing upwards. As with the other commands you have learnt so far, the turtle draws a line as it moves. So you can even use the HOME command to draw. You can draw a plus sign using the HOME command.

FD 100	FD 100
HOME	HOME
BK 100	LT 90
HOME	FD 100
RT 90	

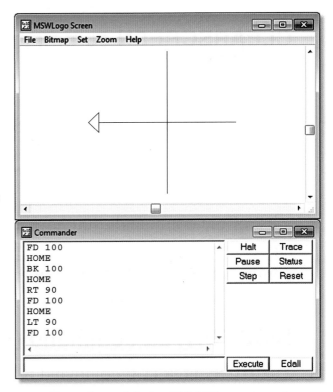

Drawing with the HOME command

105

SETH command

You can use the SETH command in place of RT and LT. This command in Logo is used to rotate the turtle. Similar to RT and LT commands, you must give a number with the SETH command. The SETH command then turns the turtle's head in the clockwise direction accordingly.

Here are some examples of SETH command.

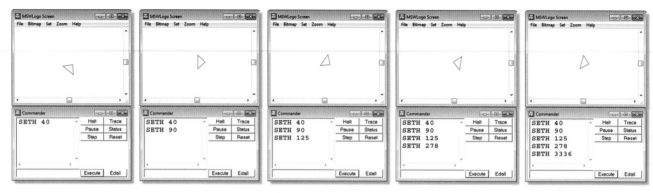

SETH command

In the SETH command, the units are not counted from the current position of the turtle as in the LT and RT commands. They are always counted from the HOME position, that is, the starting position of the turtle.

CLEARSCREEN command (CS)

The CLEARSCREEN command clears the drawing on the screen and brings the turtle back to the starting position. The short form for the CLEARSCREEN command is CS.

CLEARTEXT command (CT)

You have seen that the Recall list box in the Commander window shows you a list of the commands you have entered, along with the result of arithmetic calculations and any error messages. You can use the CLEARTEXT command to clear all the text in the Recall list box area. The short form for the CLEARTEXT command is CT.

HIDE TURTLE command (HT)

The HIDE TURTLE command is used for hiding the turtle so that you can see the drawing more clearly. Hide the turtle and then give a command like

FD 50. The turtle will still draw a line even though you cannot see the turtle on the screen. The short form for the HIDE TURTLE command is HT.

SHOW TURTLE command (ST)

After you have given the HIDE TURTLE command, you can make the turtle reappear on the screen by giving the SHOW TURTLE command. The short form for the SHOW TURTLE command is ST.

REPEAT command

With this command you can instruct Logo to execute (run) the given commands a number of times. You have to give Logo two instructions along with the REPEAT command:

- Which commands to repeat?
- How many times to repeat them?

Using this command, you can draw a square in a single step.

Drawing a Square with the REPEAT command

You can draw a square in one single step.

For this you need to give the following commands:

1. Type REPEAT 4 [FD 100 RT 90].
2. Press the **Enter** key.

BYE command

As you have learnt in the last chapter, you can also close MSWLogo using the BYE command.

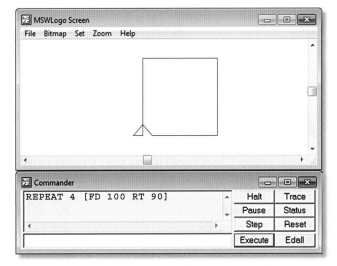

Using the REPEAT command

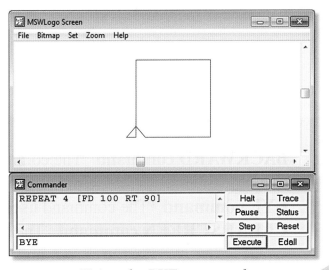

Using the BYE command

Help tips for Logo

- Capital letters don't need to be used in a command.
- Give a single space between the command and the number. For example, if you type FD 85, Logo will show you the message 'I don't know how to FD 85' so you need to type FD85.
- Always press ENTER after you have typed in a command. Otherwise, the turtle will think that you are going to give more commands and will not do anything.
- Always type the complete command before you press ENTER. For example, if you simply type FD, Logo will show you the message 'Not enough inputs to FD'.

ACTIVITY

Circle the error(s) in the given commands.

1.	BK 200	2.	FD 150
	LT 90		RT 90 FD 150
	FD 200		RT 90
	TR 90		FD 150
	CS		

GLOSSARY

BACKWARD command The command that moves the turtle in the direction opposite to the direction it is pointing.

BYE command The command used for exiting MSWLogo.

CLEARSCREEN command The command that clears the drawing on the screen and brings the turtle back to the starting position.

CLEARTEXT command The command that clears all the text in the Recall list box area.

FORWARD command   The command that moves the turtle forward in the direction in which it is pointing.

HIDE TURTLE command   The command that is used for hiding the turtle to see the drawing clearly.

HOME command   The command that brings the turtle back to its HOME position.

HOME position   This is where the turtle is at the centre of the main screen with its head pointing upwards.

LEFT command   The command that makes the turtle turn towards the left side.

Primitives   The basic commands of Logo.

REPEAT command   The command that executes (runs) the given command a given number of times.

RIGHT command   The command that makes the turtle turn towards the right side.

SETH command   The command that rotates the turtle to the right side starting from the HOME position.

SHOW TURTLE command   The command that is used for making the turtle appear on the screen again.

YOU ARE HERE

9

1. The basic commands used in MSW Logo are HOME, FORWARD, BACKWARD, LEFT, RIGHT, SETH, CLEARSCREEN, CLEARTEXT, HIDE TURTLE, SHOW TURTLE, BYE and REPEAT.

2. Logo allows you to give more than one command. You can give several commands and then press the Execute button to get the output.

3. While typing the command, leave a single space between the command and the number.

EXERCISE

A.   Identify the following commands.

1. It moves the turtle to the starting position.   ....

2. It moves the turtle forward.   ....

3. It rotates the turtle to the right side.   ....

4. It clears the Recall list box.   ....

5. It executes a command a given number of times.   ....

B. True or false?

1. The REPEAT command executes the last command again.

2. Primitives are the tools you use in Logo.

3. The BYE command helps you exit Logo.

4. You can move the turtle in a straight line only.

5. The short form for the BACKWARD command is BK.

C. Fill in the blanks with the correct item from the box.

CS	Primitives	BK 100	HOME	CLEARTEXT

1. Logo commands are known as ....
2. The .... command clears the screen and brings the turtle back to the starting position.
3. The .... command makes the turtle go back to its starting position.
4. To move the turtle 100 steps backward, you type the .... command.
5. The .... command clears Recall list box area.

D. Answer the following questions.

1. List any four commands that you can use to draw a rectangle.
2. What is the difference between the SETH command and the RT command?
3. How is CLEARSCREEN different from the CLEARTEXT command?
4. What is the command for:
    a. drawing a square in a single step.
    b. exiting Logo.
    c. bringing the turtle back to its HOME position.
    d. repeating a command a given number of times.
    e. cleaning all the text from Recall list box area?

LAB WORK

Draw the following shapes using Logo commands. Use the Repeat command wherever possible.

1.

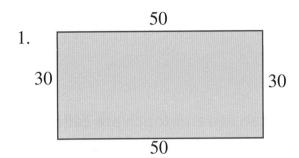

50
30
30
50

3.

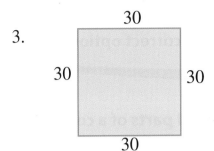

30
30
30
30

2.

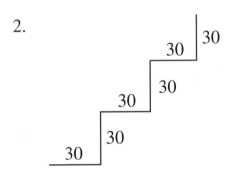

30
30
30
30
30
30

4.

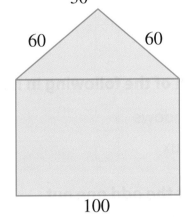

60
60
100

PROJECT WORK

Draw any 5 letters of the English alphabet in capital in MSWLogo. An example is given here for your reference.

A, H, N, T, X

Outcome: You will be able to understand the turtle movement and will be able to decide the number of steps and angles for drawing different figures.

Sample Paper

Tick (✔) the correct option.

1. **The physical parts of a computer that you can see and touch are called ....**

   a. Software ☐

   b. Hardware ☐

   c. Multimedia ☐

   d. Icons ☐

2. **Which of the following in not an example of an operating system?**

   a. Windows ☐

   b. Linux ☐

   c. MS Paint ☐

   d. Unix ☐

3. **Select the odd one out.**

   a. Start button ☐

   b. Taskbar ☐

   c. Notification area ☐

   d. Keyboard ☐

4. **Which of the following shortcut keys is used to paste copied text?**

   a. Ctrl + V ☐

   b. Ctrl + C ☐

   c. Ctrl + X ☐

   d. Ctrl + Z ☐

5. **Select the default color of the foreground color (also called Color 1) in Paint.**

   a. White ☐

   b. Black ☐

   c. Green ☐

   d. Yellow ☐

6. **Where is the Find option in MS Word 2010?**

   a. Clipboard group of File tab ☐

   b. Editing group of File tab ☐

   c. Editing group of Home tab ☐

   d. Clipboard group of Home tab ☐

7. **From the options given below, select the example of the Toggle case option available in MS Word 2010.**

a. CYBER OLYMPIAD ☐　　　c. Cyber Olympiad ☐

b. Cyber olympiad ☐　　　d. cYBER oLYMPIAD ☐

8. **Which of the following option(s) is/are correct about the Start button in Windows 7?**

a. All Programs option appears here. ☐

b. You can shut down your computer from here. ☐

c. You can open the software installed on your computer from here. ☐

d. All of the above. ☐

9. **Select the icon of the tool in Paint which can be used to draw a hexagon.**

a. ☐　　　c. ☐

b. ☐　　　d. ☐

10. **Name the tool you use for inserting text in a picture.**

a. Shapes tool ☐　　　c. Image tool ☐

b. Text tool ☐　　　d. Color picker tool ☐

11. **Identify the icon B .**

a. Underline ☐　　　c. Bold ☐

b. Strikethrough ☐　　　d. Italic ☐

12. **What is the function of shortcut key Ctrl + R in Paint?**

a. Used to rotate or flip an image ☐

b. Used to resize and skew an image ☐

c. Used to zoom in and zoom out on an image ☐

d. Used to enlarge an image ☐

13. **Which of the following components does not belong to Tux Paint?**

a. Toolbar pane ☐　　　c. Selector pane ☐

b. Colors group ☐　　　d. File tab ☐

14. Which of the following Tux Paint tools is used to draw lines?

a. ☐

c. ☐

b. ☐

d. None of the above ☐

15. Which of the following tools is represented by the Linux Penguin?

a. MS Word ☐

c. Tux Paint ☐

b. Windows 10 ☐

d. MS Paint ☐

16. Select the part(s) of the MSWLogo Turtle.

a. Head ☐

c. Both A and B ☐

b. Tail ☐

d. None of the above ☐

17. Which of the following is not a Control button in MSWLogo?

a. Halt ☐

c. Status ☐

b. Trace ☐

d. Stop ☐

18. Identify the computer icon.

a. ☐

c. ☐

b. ☐

d. ☐

19. Select the button you can use to close a window.

a. ☐

c. ☐

b. ☐

d. ☐

20. Select the shortcut key used for deleting a file permanently.

a. Shift + Del ☐

c. Explorer Key + Del ☐

b. Explorer Key + Tab ☐

d. Shift + Backspace ☐